THE MAN WHO DANCED AROUND THE WORLD

MR. JAMES E WOOD JR

Getting Started

It was the end of June 1992 when I packed up my essential personal stuff, left my lifetime field of work as a manager of engineering services for a major steel company, and entered retirement. To say I had no idea what to do with this newfound freedom would be untruthful. I was going to do all kinds of "things." Playing golf, bridge, eating out, and yard work came to mind. Not very exciting in the long view. Here I was, single, with two great, employed, and happily married sons, and the time and means to attack almost any new activity I chose. Through a quirk of fate, some unbelievable luck, and a bit of the old corporate drive, I became a cruise-line dance host.

One evening in 1984, I was having a pleasant conversation with my friend Sue, a single mother raising five children. I was sort of a fill-in support system for her, and she was my sounding board for dealing with my new single life. I had mentioned that I had made some new friends since my divorce in 1978, but I would like to make more. Sue told me that she'd read about a dance studio nearby that was offering three free lessons and maybe that would be good for me. I said I didn't want to learn to dance, just make new friends. But she stressed that dancing attracts a different set of people I was unlikely to meet otherwise. So I enrolled.

The only dancing I had ever done was the obligatory fake stuff at weddings. Jeri, wife of the studio owner, took me under her wing, and in no time she had me dancing pretty well. I participated in their showcases, and several ladies requested me as an escort to dance functions. Eventually dancing became a big chunk of my social life. Sue had been dead on. I acquired new friends plus a new set of social skills. Little did I suspect that this was just my first step.

It was March 1989 when I received a call in my office at the steel company, and on the other end of the line was a gentleman named Ted who introduced himself as a "placement agent" from Florida, for dance hosts. He told me that a friend of mine, Carol, had recommended me as a candidate for hosting on Mississippi riverboats. Carol was a single schoolteacher and a successful writer of cookbooks. We had met in a singles club, and she was aware of my newly acquired dancing skills. She spent her summer vacations on cruise lines as an arts and crafts teacher and used Ted for her assignments.

I listened to his pitch, and it sounded pretty good. I was able to get two consecutive weeks' vacation, and we agreed on dates that would work. The deal was that I would get free transportation to and from the riverboat in exchange for paying him a placement fee. My first assignment was from St. Louis to New Orleans on the Mississippi Queen. It went flawlessly except for the fact that my cha-cha skills were nearly nonexistent. (I actually headed for the men's room whenever one was played.) This was my first taste of the opulence and grandeur of this kind of vacationing. The food was plentiful and delicious, the guests were affluent yet friendly, and I felt that the line appreciated my efforts. That was confirmed when Ted called when I returned home and said I had passed the host test and he looked forward to placing me on other river cruises.

Armed with this endorsement, I learned of other hosting assignments and explored them. I worked some of the resorts in the Catskills of New York. Since these were weekend affairs, I could easily fit that into my social schedule without interfering with my work. I used vacation time to do more riverboat hosting in 1990 and 1991 through Ted. On the last of these trips my fellow host, Sherman, from San Francisco, told me I belonged on the oceans as a dance host. I told him I was still working for the steel company, but he encouraged me to put in an application with Royal Cruise Line, the one he worked for. He offered to endorse, me so I said, "Why not." He also provided me with the name of another agent, this one in Chicago, who supplied hosts to the big cruise lines.

It so happened that in March 1992, my employer offered me an early retirement. I accepted, and not long thereafter called the placement agent in Chicago that Sherman had recommended and inquired how I would go about getting assignments. The lady I spoke to said that she would be conducting interviews and dance tests in the New York area in several months. But I didn't want to wait that long. I asked when the next interviews were being held, and she said that weekend in Chicago. I told her I would fly out if it was all right with her. She laughed and said if I wanted to invest in the trip and an overnight stay, she would be glad to include me with the other twelve men she'd be auditioning. So I grabbed a late Friday flight to Chicago, rented a car, found a motel, and was at the doorstep of the dance studio the next morning. I came away with assignments for consecutive transatlantic cruises out of and back to New York, leaving five days after my June retirement.

Buoyed by that success, I placed a call to Royal Cruise Line to ask the status of the application I had previously submitted. I was finally put in touch with a young lady who said someone would call me within the week. Frankly, I thought this was a put-off because Sherman had said that Royal was the top of the heap for hosts. As I hung up, I was only mildly confident I would hear from them. But about a week later, a gentleman named Bruce called back. He was a Royal employee, not an agent, and he explained that he did have my application and the endorsement from Sherman. He asked me to come to San Francisco for an interview. I asked him what time could he see me the next day. Bruce said I must have misunderstood. He was in San Francisco, and I was in Allentown, Pennsylvania. I said, "No, I understand perfectly; what time tomorrow can you see me?" He laughed, and we continued to chat about all kinds of things. As he drew the conversation to a close, I once again asked about a time for tomorrow. He said that a trip to San Francisco wouldn't be necessary, and if I didn't hear from someone in his office within a week to call him personally. Three days later I had my first host assignment to the Mexican Riviera, with Royal Cruise Line, scheduled for early November 1992. I was on my way! My next phone call was to my tailor with a request to visit him for a fitting for a tuxedo, white dinner jacket, and other necessary formal attire. Previously I had rented the formal clothing I required.

In the mid-1980s, it became apparent to the now defunct Royal Cruise Line that there were an increasing number of unescorted ladies taking cruises. Many were widows fulfilling the dream they had shared with departed husbands. Socializing is a great part of cruising, and that includes dancing. To accommodate and encourage these ladies and other unescorted women, Royal sought out retired men who could dance and interact socially with their guests. In exchange, these gentlemen received a free cruise. As time went by, the idea caught on and other cruise lines began employing hosts as well. Most of these lines used agents to find them. Although different lines use different titles, we're all essentially dance hosts. We're typically single, fifty years or older, able to dance well and generally like people and travel. As years passed, hosts were asked or volunteered to do other cruise-related activities such as manning the lights for shows, helping with disembarkation for passengers, escorting land tours, and hosting a table for dinner.

Since I started hosting in 1989, I have danced and socialized across six continents, in 161 countries, on fifteen different cruise ships, with seven different cruise lines, touching over five hundred ports of call. As a reminder of just how many places I have been, a world map resides in my basement game room punctured with a pin for every city, town, and hamlet whose streets I have trodden.

I can look at that map and recall details of all those places, but it's surprising what those memories mainly revolve around. Not so much the port where we landed. Not the tree lined roads with the glorious country sides. Not the impressive buildings with ornate architecture. Not even the glaciers. No, it's the people I met along the way. The "strangers" from everywhere whom I shared those sights with are the catalysts for the recollections that make up this memoir. If I had a bumper sticker for my life, it would read: "Places are wonderful, but places with people are better." It is hard to pinpoint when, during this wonderful second career that thought occurred to me. As a friend once said, "You're stating the obvious with an air of discovery." He, of course, was correct.

That being my premise, here is a collection of vignettes dealing with the people I have met along the way. Some are quite detailed, others are very short, but I believe they all make a point. Though as dance hosts we concentrate on unescorted ladies, we also interact with couples and single gentlemen as well as crew, staff and, of course, the people ashore in the countries we visit. Just as fascinating as the people themselves are the behaviors they exhibit. Some are funny, some sad, some confusing, some touching, but all are honest and have touched me in some way. In my mind most contain a moral or lesson worth remembering. I hope you enjoy my adventures with these wonderful and interesting people as much as I have.

Two Sisters

My first ocean cruise came in 1992, from New York to Dover, England. I was on my first dance host assignment and having trouble finding my backside with both hands. The ship was huge. Its smokestack reminded me of a battleship gun. Somehow I got through boarding, found my cabin, and stowed my gear. I was already using nautical jargon. With difficulty, I found the cruise director's office and introduced myself. I was handed the schedule for the day and given a ten-second briefing and sent on my way. I got it. I was to use all those wonderful adaptive skills that I possessed and try to survive.

At the first dance session of the evening, I met the other three hosts, introduced myself, and learned that they too were very short on hosting experience. "Dance, stupid, dance," was the only thing I felt would relieve my sudden urge to find the nearest restroom. There appeared to be several unescorted ladies, so I selected a likely candidate and asked if she would care to dance this waltz. She graciously accepted, and we did a passable imitation of a waltz.

She told me her name was Shirley and that she and her sister, Rosemary, were on the cruise together. I now had my second dance partner, if I could just get Shirley back to her seat before one of the other hosts found "the sister." Luckily, I found myself on the floor with Rosemary. Before either of us realized it, the band was playing a semblance of a fast foxtrot or slow swing. I later found out it was a dance called the "quickstep." I really faked that one as other couples whizzed by us. The quickstep was not a dance I had learned from my dance studio back home. I made a mental note to correct that if I ever survived this. The rest of that first evening and the many other ladies I danced with are still a blur, but somehow I got through it all, as did my fellow hosts.

The next morning, as I strolled the deck, I came across the sisters. They asked me to sit and chat a while. They were English, and the three of us had fun getting acquainted. Turns out Rosemary and I shared the same birth date and birth year—Halloween, 1933. Wow, I found my twin on the second dance.

Sister Shirley was four years younger, and her deceased husband had been a member of the Buckingham Palace Guard.

Within a few minutes, it became clear to me that I had found two fun ladies to spend some of my time with. They said my accent was interesting, and we explored the actual and perceived differences between the "Brits" and "Yanks." I'm not sure we came to any profound conclusions, but I do know that were it not for these two "strangers," my first cruise-line host experience would likely not have led to a second. Their own self-assurance bathed me with confidence, and I truly had fun. It's been over twenty years since that meeting, and we corresponded from time to time for a few years. Though we have lost touch with one another, I will always remember Shirley and Rosemary providing my baptism into the dance host religion.

ROOKIE

My "check out" cruise with Royal Cruise Line came in November 1992, and I was a little nervous. Though I had some hosting experience, this particular line was new to me. It was to be a ten-day cruise along the Mexican Riviera. I found the pier in San Francisco, where the ship was berthed, negotiated the boarding process, and moved into my cabin. I was running a little late since my flight had been delayed. I quickly unpacked and settled in. A schedule for the day was on my desk, and I saw that dance hosts and other ship personnel were to be introduced at the evening show. I laid out the proper clothes, shaved, showered, and got dressed for my first big event. I looked sharp in my blue blazer, white slacks, white shirt, and nautical tie.

With a little direction, I found the showroom. It was packed with passengers, and in one corner stood five gentlemen dressed like me whom I took to be my dance host colleagues. I introduced myself and tried to remember their names, but all too quickly the cruise director started the proceedings. From their casual demeanor, it was apparent that these fellows were seasoned hosts. Each also appeared to be at least ten years older than I. When it was our time to be introduced, we lined up to walk down the center aisle to the stage. We were told to give our first name and hometown, then pass the microphone to the next person. Since there seemed to be a pecking order, I fell in line at the rear. The cruise director handed the mike to the first host: Tony, Walnut Creek, California; then Bill, San Diego, California; Arnold, Sacramento, California; Marcus, San Jose, California; Victor, Santa Barbara, California: then me: Jim, Allentown, Pennsylvania. (California 5-Pennsylvania 1).

The rest of the evening I kept my eye on my fellow hosts to see how things were handled. I didn't notice them doing anything unusual, so I continued to do the job as I felt it should be done. Most of the hosts were cautiously friendly, except for one. Arnold from Sacramento seemed downright hostile. I tried to figure out what I had done to cross him. The ladies seemed happy with us, and the time flew by.

I continued to follow my assignments and chatted from time to time with my fellow hosts; that is, all except Arnold. At the end of the fourth night, Tony, whom I correctly pegged as the lead dance host, asked me if I would join him for a nightcap. We made small talk as we sipped our gin and tonics. Then Tony finally said, "The home office told me they were putting a rookie on board, and they wanted me to watch you and report back." I asked if he had any advice for me. He said, "Just keep doing what you are doing, rookie, and you will be fine." He asked if I was having any problems. I said I wasn't, except I wondered why the other hosts seemed tentative with me, and why Arnold was a little nasty. He laughed. Since I was younger, they were guessing I was the nephew of some bigwig for the cruise line, so they were being cautious. I assured Tony that was not the case. He said he would tell the home office that I was a keeper. Tony must have reported out to the other hosts, because afterward they were much friendlier. All except Arnold, who finally asked how a guy from Pennsylvania could possibly become a host for a

West Coast cruise line. I told him, "Because I'm good." That was the end of that.

Since then I have sailed with Tony probably twenty times over the years and we became good friends. When he told me he was thinking of hanging up his dance shoes, I told him I could never repay him for the courtesies he showed me when I was starting out. "Yes you can," he told me. "Find some rookie, and help him when he needs it." I did and I have.

Ghost Host

In the spring of 1993, Royal Cruise Line assigned me once again as a dance host for a ten-day trip along the Mexican Riviera. In order to make passengers aware that dance hosts were aboard, all six of us were introduced, along with other staff, at some first night festivity. We were dressed in "the uniform" as it was called in those days—a blue blazer, white trousers, white shoes, and socks, white shirt, and a nautical tie. Royal Cruise Line actually originated the dance host program, and it was impressive to see so many gentlemen lined up on a stage. On a cruise of this length, we would don this uniform four or five times. In addition, there were usually two formal nights when we were dressed nearly alike in our tuxedos and bow ties. Other evenings we wore suits or sports jackets. The dress code was designed to give the dance hosts a special and identifiable look. As a rookie, I was advised to always dress one cut above the passengers and to always wear my name badge.

On this particular cruise, I knew only one of the other hosts, a fellow named Tony. The other four gentlemen were new to me. Later in the evening on that first night, I looked around the room during a pause in the dancing and counted seven "uniforms," including myself. I thought I had miscounted until Tony approached me and asked if another host had boarded late and was unable to make the introduction ceremony. I said I didn't know, but agreed that there were seven guys in the signature blue blazer and white pants on the dance floor. We figured that if someone had joined late, we would meet him at the entertainment meeting that was scheduled for the next morning. So we didn't give it another thought and went back to doing our job.

The next morning at the meeting, there were just the six of us. Neither Tony nor I could explain it. And later that day at the dance class, all six of us were present again. Tony and I agreed we must have been seeing things.

That evening at the captain's welcome party, the dress was formal. Many unescorted ladies, couples, and a few single gentlemen were in attendance, and the dancing went on until well past midnight. All the hosts were extremely busy.

Two evenings later, it was once again uniform night, and the dance floor was as crowded as ever. I was dancing the last dance of a set with a very attractive lady, Dolores, from Tucson whom I had met earlier in the cruise. When the band took a break, she asked me to join her at her table. We sat down and exchanged pleasantries, but then Dolores got very serious. She told me that she had a huge complaint about one of the dance hosts, and she didn't know what do about it. She said his language was highly suggestive, and in dance class and also during the evening sets his dancing position was much too familiar. She added that another lady had experienced the same behavior and had actually stopped dancing because of it.

Trying to be as gracious as possible, I told Dolores that I would intercede on her behalf if she would point out the offending host. As I mentioned, I was a relatively new host, so I wasn't sure exactly what I'd do, but I figured I could always enlist Tony's help. He was an old pro, and between the two of us I was confident we'd be able to figure it out.

"So, who is it?" I asked. "That man right there," said Dolores, pointing her finger across the room at a gentleman who, to my amazement, was dressed exactly like a dance host but who was not one of us.

He was our "number seven." This wily fellow was passing himself off as a host in order to get closer to the ladies. I immediately told Dolores that this "wannabe" wasn't a real host, but now I was in a bind. I had promised to act on her behalf, as any gentleman would do under the circumstances. But the problem was that this fellow was a paying passenger, who had to be respected. My years of dealing with people had taught me that no matter how willing one is to correct a bad situation, it is very easy to make it worse. One cannot directly solve all problems. The solution, it seemed to me was to enlist the help of the appropriate onboard official. Tony agreed, and together we assembled the facts as we knew them, informed the other dance hosts of our intentions, and passed our concerns up the line to Charles, the cruise director. As it turned out, Charles had already received myriad complaints against this same passenger.

At our next opportunity, we made sure all the unescorted ladies knew who the legitimate hosts were. After all, no competent dance host wants to be painted with the brush of a louse. The cruise director or some other official apparently took action because the "ghost host" absented himself from many functions for the rest of the cruise, and when he did appear, he was the paragon of virtuous behavior. I know Dolores had no further complaints. It goes without saying that the six of us dance hosts kept an eye out for this guy throughout the remainder of the cruise and even on future cruises.

For all I know, on some ship somewhere, the ghost host may still sail. While part of me admired his gumption and creativity, dance hosting, after all, is a job for a professional.

Spin Off

About two years after I began my dance host career on the Mississippi riverboats, another opportunity arose. This time it was as a dance host at resorts in the Catskill Mountains of New York. On a lark, my buddy Gus and I went to one of these resorts for a dance weekend. There were about six hundred people there. The music was good, the entertainment was excellent, and there were plenty of ladies to dance with. At a break late on the first evening, a young lady named Phyllis asked to speak with me. She represented the company that sponsored these events and had an all-business look on her face.

"Did you notice there were about twenty men with name tags who were dancing with the ladies?" she asked. "Yes," I replied. "I assumed they were dance hosts brought on to dance with unescorted ladies." She said that was exactly right, and asked whether I was interested in working for her. The company ran four dance weekends every year. Each was held at some venue in the Catskills and was popular with singles and couples from the New York, New Jersey, Connecticut, and Massachusetts areas. The hosts paid a nominal fee for the whole weekend, and they received a shared hotel room, all meals, and free access to the other hotel amenities. Not a bad deal for a long weekend, I thought, so I agreed, and we exchanged contact information.

On my first assignment, I found that several things were decidedly different from riverboat hosting. For example, each lady was allowed to have two consecutive dances with a host instead of just one. Finding another lady was never a problem since they sat or stood at the edge of the dance floor and would jump up or grab you as you departed the dance floor. So much for escorting your partner to her seat! (She probably didn't even have one anyway.)

Most of the ladies were also very accomplished dancers. Many had taken lessons at home, so I had to pull out all my skills to keep up with them. Additionally, we hosts were to sit with single ladies at a table near the portable dance floors for lunch and dinner because there was constant music for dancing then as well. Since the tables seated eight people, many times it would be all women and me. As you can imagine, it was challenging to eat. About the time a mouthful of food got to my lips, a lady from another table might tap me on the shoulder. This was certainly different from the casual meals and conversation I had enjoyed on the river. The music played into the late hours, and we hosts did a lot of dancing. Thankfully, after each assigned hour of dance there was a one-hour break. That was a lifesaver. Did I mention there was afternoon dancing and dance classes in the morning as well?

Another huge difference was that my previous hosting assignments had frowned upon fraternization with guests. Not so here. Opportunities for after-hour "coffee" were frequent. The invitations were discreet, but you would have had to be very naïve not to recognize them. One of the fellow hosts I befriended was Ed. We shared war stories, and it was no surprise to run into him aboard a ship about three years later. He is a real man's man, and we became very good friends and confidants. The whole Catskill experience was certainly different than what I was used to. The typical behavior of the land dancers was much more aggressive (both men and women) than I found at sea. I continued to do this Catskill gig for perhaps five years, and I had a ball each and every time. I found these getaways to be well run and upbeat, and I'll always remember these weekend dances as being a worthwhile addition to my dance host experiences.

MISDIRECTION

I was on a team of six hosts on a round-trip cruise out of Fort
Lauderdale, Florida, to the Caribbean. I was by far the youngest
host with the least experience, so naturally my colleagues and
the ladies were watching me pretty closely. We happened to have
three or four younger women on this cruise as well—all very
attractive, I might add.

After the first night's dancing, two of my fellow hosts, Clark
and Roger, who were seasoned, speculated that I had a little thing
going with one of these ladies—Joan, who hailed from Tyler, Texas.
Though that was far from the truth, over the next day or so, they
and some of the ladies I danced with became convinced that there
was some hanky-panky going on. Though there was not a grain of
truth to their suspicions about "Texas," there was a lady from Iowa
named Charlotte, who was traveling with her mother, whom I did
have an eye on. She admitted to an interest in me as well. Though
I didn't expect to deviate from the frowned-upon extra-attention

guideline, I was permitted to legitimately spend time with her and her mother ashore or over cocktails. This suited Charlotte and me fine. But what was I to do about the perception that my attentions were directed at the Texas gal?

I determined it would be unfair to avoid Joan in an attempt to defuse the perception of my fellow hosts. After some thought, I decided to make no effort to change the way I was treating Joan, though such attention would continue to be read as special treatment. I figured that those who were watching me would focus their attention on that situation while overlooking my real target.

At cruise end, the two hosts who were positive I was doing some "after-hours dancing" asked me how I had managed to pull off my extracurricular activities with the lady from Texas. I just smiled and told them they were not the only clever guys aboard. Let them think what they wanted. Over the years, I have sailed with these two hosts, Clark and Roger, many times, and never once have they failed to ask me how I pulled off that coup with Texas Joan. The misdirection technique had worked to perfection and was a useful tool to have in my social kit should I find the desire to pull it out at some date in the future.

ALFRED THE GREAT

It was a hot, sticky, windless morning as the ship docked in Mombasa, Kenya. Nevertheless, I could hardly wait to get ashore. Today I would be one of three escorts for a group of fifty-eight guests going on a one-day safari. Our transportation would be twelve minibuses, each holding up to six persons plus the driver, who also doubled as the guide. One escort would be with the first minibus, another with the sixth minibus, and I on the last one.

After assuring everyone was aboard and getting the signal to move out in caravan style, I jumped into the last bus. My driver was Alfred Omondi, and we had no other passengers. I thought this odd until Alfred assured me in excellent English, with a slight British accent, that the last bus was a spare. If a breakdown should occur, the passengers from that bus could be transferred to ours, and no one would be inconvenienced. Though not a foolproof plan, it showed someone was thinking ahead.

So for the one and a half hours it took to get to the Tsavo East Game Reserve, I had a personal tour guide. I asked many questions about Kenya and the sights along the way. Alfred answered them all and threw in other information regarding his country and the safari. For the whole day at the game preserve, Alfred pointed out the animals and sights to me as we brought up the rear of the minibus column, each with its raised roof to facilitate observation, cameras, and binoculars. Alfred spotted and identified a pride of lions here, a tribe of baboons over there, plus giraffes, elephants, gazelles, water buffalo, wildebeests, termite homes, iguanas, birds of all kinds, ostriches, and zebras. He seemed to know exactly where to look and when to stop to see the best sights. It was almost as though someone had placed these creatures there for our benefit.

We got to know each other pretty well, and by day's end we were laughing and having a wonderful time. The rest of the passengers on tour cooperated, and I had very few official situations to handle except to make sure my people count was correct. This gave me more free time to benefit from Alfred's expertise. We had our pictures taken together, and I learned that Alfred was the sole supporter of a wife, three children, one brother, two sisters, a mother, a father, and one uncle. Quite a feat on a meager tour guide salary.

When we reached the dock at the end of the day, I was a happy camper. I thanked Alfred for the day and bestowed a very generous tip, both for his guiding and, I must admit, his circumstance. I traded addresses with him and promised to send him a copy of the picture of us when I got home.

As promised, I later wrote Alfred a letter, enclosed the photo, and added a little money to help with his finances. About six weeks after that, I received a note from Alfred.

He wrote, "I've this opportunity to thank you very much on receiving letter and kindly heart to remember my empty pocket. The cash you mailed also I received. I wish you plus your family happy staying and hopefully to see you again in Kenya. I and the family are doing okay health wise. Only the season is low due to no clients coming for tours of which the cash helped me on a big stuck. Thank you very much.

Hope to read from you again,
Yours friendly, Alfred Omondi

I have read this letter repeatedly, and each time I see this wonderful, bright-eyed Kenyan, with his flashing smile and proud
demeanor. My guess is that he had the benefit of some schooling
in his youth. I judged him to be in his thirties. I know I will write
to him again. I am overwhelmed by Alfred's and his family's apparent need. The clincher is that he is out there trying, unlike some I
have seen around the world. On that basis alone, Alfred will continue to get my respect, along with my heartfelt assistance.

Jill-Ted

One of the "no-no's" of being a dance host aboard cruise ships is treating one lady more favorably than any of the others. This is intended to see that all ladies who dance get equal opportunity to do so. Naturally, this policy carries over to all social activities. For instance, dining alone with one lady at one of the specialty restaurants is taboo. It goes without saying that inviting a lady to a host cabin or accompanying her to hers is a threshold a host would be smart not to cross. Now let me tell you of a lady who didn't quite agree with how this policy is administered by the hosts and how I tried to handle that.

Her name was Jill and she hailed from the northwest, Seattle, I think. On our first dance on a twelve-day cruise out of Miami, I knew instinctively that her middle name was *Trouble*. Packed into an expensive, chic, semiformal outfit, her five-foot six-inch frame belied her age, which I judged to be early sixties. Her slim waist, ample chest, and big smile would disarm most people, but I have learned over years of meeting people that first impressions need to be tempered with a little time. In Jill's case it was very little time. On our third dance of the evening, near quitting time, she got inside my comfort zone on a slow dance, and what my imagination had guessed about her physical attributes she confirmed with her body press. She suggested that we go for a drink. I declined, using the excuse that I was escorting a tour the next day and needed a good night's rest. With a wink she said, "We'll do *it* another time soon."

The next evening this blond bombshell was seated right in front at the dance venue and, to no one's surprise, my fellow dance hosts were hovering around her. This was good news because I had planned to use them to deflect any extra attention I might get from Jill. From the looks on the other unescorted ladies' faces, I could tell that Jill's presence was not particularly welcome, though they couldn't do much about it. She ignored the other hosts, however, and asked me for a slow dance. This was not the normal protocol. We gentleman normally asked the ladies to dance. That way we could assure, as best we can, that no one got left out. On the other hand, I could not very well refuse her, since she was a paying passenger. It was on this dance that she whispered to me what her plan for me was on this cruise. I pretended to think she was joking and that I didn't grasp the full meaning of her words. But inside I was wondering how I was going to handle this for nine more days.

I fell back on a tactic I had used successfully a few times in hosting. I could not ignore Jill. She deserved to have her turn with me as well as with the other hosts in dancing, so I decided to ask her to dance only when they played a faster number like the cha-cha, swing, mambo, or samba. That way I'd steer clear of the foxtrot, rumba, tango, and any other dances where the bodies are closer.

On my initial swing with her, she smiled and said, "You can dance, but you can't run." I gave her the old quizzical look and played dumb once again. Meanwhile, my fellow hosts were getting the cold shoulder from her, though in fairness, they were trying their best to have their turn to dance with her. This is when I first became aware that martinis were her drink of choice—many of them—but never so many that she wasn't fully in control.

Next evening it was the same, but during the break she followed me out of the dance floor and caught up with me as I was boarding an elevator to go to my cabin. As the doors closed behind just the two of us, she explained in no uncertain terms what she had in mind for me. I continued with the dumb approach, but I knew I would soon have to make a choice whether to uphold my contract of non-fraternization or not.

I needed to test the outside waters to see if any of the hosts had noticed the extra attention I thought I was getting from Jill. But they told me that they didn't notice any behaviors on my part or hers that sent a message of special treatment to the other ladies. I was concerned about the other ladies since they were very astute. One host said confidentially that if he were to get even a hint of interest from Jill, he might take a chance on violating his contract. The penalty for getting caught with a passenger under cover, so to speak, is debarkation at the next port and a trip home at your own expense. I later explained this to Jill with the aside that I was flattered by the attention, but I couldn't afford to put myself in that position, but the innuendos, sex talk, and body rubs still continued throughout the rest of the cruise. On the last evening Jill told me, "You are one of the nicest guys I have ever met, and you are the dumbest s.o.b. I have ever known." Trying to soothe the situation, I told her that maybe we could exchange addresses and get together off the ship. She killed me with, "I want you *now* and *here*, not sometime at home." It was a relief that Jill left the ship the next morning. I must admit, on that last night, I was sorely tempted to fulfill her wants, especially since she would be gone by daybreak.

The whole thing reminded me of a graph I once saw of a Sexual Urgency Curve (SUC). One's sexual urgency increases as available time left decreases. One's fear of getting caught decreases as available time decreases. The last evening of the cruise is the opportunity of last resort.

About thirteen months later, on another cruise, Jill was again aboard. On our first dance, she asked me if we were going to go through the same crap we did the last time we met. I asked her what she meant by that. She looked at me, shook her head, and said, "You're still a dumb s.o.b."

I BEG YOUR PARDON

As I strolled alone in the old section of San Juan, Puerto Rico, an elderly man asked me for two dollars to buy breakfast. I gave it to him and immediately kicked myself for doing so. I continued my walk, observing the sites when I bumped into the same man about thirty minutes later and asked him, somewhat tartly, how his breakfast was. He withdrew from his pocket about seventy-five cents in change, smiled, and thanked me for my kindness.

I noticed that a nearby policeman had seen our exchange, so I asked about this man. He told me he knew this man and I could not have invested in a better cause. Apparently, the man had been forced from his house by family, and was trying to right himself. There is a lot of poverty in the world, and it is common to see people begging in the places I travel. It's always presented a moral dilemma for me. Tour guides will tell you, "Don't give them money because it only encourages them."

In China, for instance, they say, "Everyone has a job if they want one, so don't give money to those who beg."

I understand the rationale behind not helping these people, but I also think there can be exceptions. Many of the beggars are elderly, handicapped, or seem undernourished. Others are very young and persistent. In every case, I find myself having to make an instant decision about whether to help or not. Sometimes I help them out because they seem truly needy, other times it is just an easy way to get rid of them. On other occasions, I just ignore their presence. There doesn't seem to be a pattern to how I react, it is always just that—a reaction. The one thing I have noticed is that I tend to remember some of these encounters.

I'll not soon forget the little boy in Varanasi, India, who walked with me wordlessly holding my pants leg for five minutes until I finally gave him a dollar. He pocketed it and attached himself similarly to a lady not ten feet away from me.

Neither will I forget being overwhelmed by three gypsy women in Barcelona, Spain, who would have stripped me bare, had I not angrily shushed them away.

The poor man lying in the railway station in Mumbai, India, appeared too weak to even make an effort to beg. All who passed him looked the other way, including the policeman twirling his nightstick.

After witnessing these and many other similar situations around the world, I would have thought I would become immune to the plight of the beggars, but not so. My feelings still are touched, albeit for an instant, and I guess I will continue at least to make a conscious decision as to the level of my help, if any.

You're Mine

Early in 1994, I left San Francisco on the first of a series of cruises into the Pacific Ocean, with the first stop being Honolulu, Hawaii. We eight hosts were standing at the ready on the first evening for the standard introductions by the cruise director. We were really upbeat in our blue-blazered "uniforms," and for good reason. Normally, we expected to share a cabin with one of our fellow hosts, but on this particular cruise the ship was not full, so we each had our own cabin. This was a rare occurrence, so we were happy, and it showed.

On the signal of the cruise director, Michael, we marched to the stage and recited our names and hometowns. To much applause, we exited the stage and headed up one of the aisles that led out of the showroom. I was seventh in line, and as I passed the center of the room I noticed, out of the corner of my eye, a lady exit her aisle seat and follow us. As we hosts congregated and quickly made sure we had our first assignments for the evening straight, the lady approached and asked for a word with me. I took her aside and asked how I might be of service to her. She blew me away when she said, "My travel agent told me that I would have my own host on this cruise, and I'm choosing you." At first I thought she was kidding, but it soon became evident that she wasn't.

After telling one of the hosts I would be along in a minute, I explained to my new friend, Sandy, as kindly as I could, that this was not the way things worked. Though I was flattered with her choice, I told her I could not be hers exclusively as she had been led to believe. Her shoulders sagged and, with a feeble thank you, she slowly walked away. My gut told me two things: I was not going to share this with my seven buddies, and I was certain I had not heard the end of this encounter. I could still envision her as I hurried off to join my colleagues. Five-foot-seven, slender, blue eyes, strawberry blond hair, and around sixty years of age was my quick perception of this charming lady with a Midwestern accent.

Sure enough, early next morning brought a call from the cruise director seeking a consultation with me. I related the incident exactly as it had happened, and he agreed that is what the lady had told him. He then said we had a big problem. The travel agent who had made the promise was responsible for a whole lot of business for the cruise line. He certainly made his point when he added, "You and I have to find a way to fix this." As I pondered the dilemma, he dismissed me with, "Try your very best to make the lady feel really special." His emphasis on "really special" was not lost on me.

Armed with this new assignment, I sized up the group of ladies we danced with and, when the situation allowed, and without neglecting anybody, I was able to slip in an extra dance or two with Sandy. I even arranged to have breakfast with her some mornings and prevailed upon the maître d' to place her at the table that I hosted for dinner. When we made port in Honolulu, another host and I took her to lunch at the Aloha Towers, complete with mai tais. I must admit, she certainly was pleasant company. I engaged Sandy in conversation at every opportunity, and she seemed to feel comfortable talking to me about her life at home. A recent divorcee, her social life was nearly non-existent, and she hardly dated at all, she related.

At cruise end in Papetee, Tahiti, a smiling Sandy disembarked. The cruise director thanked me for handling the whole thing delicately and said he felt no damage was done. He added that we both had done the best we could under the circumstances. With a wry smile, he asked if having my own cabin on this cruise came in handy. Though I had not paid that kind of special attention to Sandy, I couldn't resist a wink as I said, "You don't want to know."

AN EXPERT HANDICAPPER

It had been a very long flight from my home in Allentown, Pennsylvania, to Singapore. The good news was that I flew in a day early, had a wonderful dinner, and was quartered in a hotel for the night. The next day I collected my gear, checked out, and found the bus that was to transport about twenty passengers and me to the ship for a ten-day cruise ending in Hong Kong.

Among the passengers was a stunning redhead in a wheelchair. With the assistance of the bus driver and me, she managed to board the bus and seat herself in one of the front rows reserved for handicapped persons. She motioned for me to sit beside her. Normally, we dance hosts would head for the rear of the bus in deference to the paying passengers, but in this case I made an exception.

On the twenty-minute ride, I learned that her name was Twyla, she was sixty-six, and she hailed from Lexington, Kentucky. In a soft southern drawl, she told me she was a retired veterinarian and had lost her husband to cancer some eight years earlier. A quick second marriage had not worked out, but her two children still remained close to her. I was beginning to get more information than I cared for, but I listened attentively as she told me of her work with racehorses and her social position within the Sport of Kings Society.

I was finally able to tell her that I was one of the dance hosts, but before I could go much further, she said, "Well then, we must have a dance or so." I said, "Of course, it would be my pleasure."

We arrived at the pier, and I helped her off the bus. A porter from the ship had retrieved her wheelchair, and she was rushed through the security screening, the boarding paperwork, and was out of sight within minutes.

Later that evening when I entered the showroom for dancing, there was Twyla sitting down front, sans wheelchair. She signaled me toward her and said she would love to dance. The music began, and I offered her my arm. She gracefully exited her seat, and we slowly took to the floor. The haltering gait I had expected had somehow disappeared. Being mindful of her disability, I began a delicate attempt at a basic rumba. After about fifteen seconds, she asked me if I knew anything more than the basic box step. I led her into a few rumba routines, and she did not miss a step. Apparently, her inability to walk had miraculously been healed, and thereafter throughout the cruise she seemed fine to me.

On the day of disembarkation I saw Twyla and wished her a safe journey home. No doubt it would be safe because she was once again being pushed in her wheelchair and was at the head of the line as she awaited assistance down the gangway. My guess is that the wheelchair was her constant companion for her trip home.

I Won't Dance...Don't
Ask Me

The most important function of a dance host is to find unescorted ladies who like to dance. The goal is to give those ladies the same full experience of a cruise that is available to married or coupled women. The rationale is based on the solid business principle that these ladies may very well book another cruise if they have an overall good experience, including dancing while aboard. On the surface, this may not seem like an insurmountable problem, but it can get tricky. Many times a host will see what appears to be an unescorted lady sitting by herself during the pre-show dancing set. It is, of course, embarrassing to ask one of those ladies to dance, only to have her tell you she is waiting for her husband. Usually, it is more embarrassing for the lady than the host. It can happen that the husband is in the men's room or in the casino until show time while his wife saves him his seat.

Since most passengers know about the hosts and their duties, such ladies may assume that sooner or later they will be asked to dance if it appears they're unescorted. Then the fun begins, because many times a lady will try to send the host a nonverbal message that she does not want to dance. The following are some non-verbal clues I've seen. I have come up with code names for them.

(Room Perusing) She'll pretend to be looking around the room for someone. She may do this sitting, half-raised out of her seat, or fully standing.

(Chair Cuddling) A lady will put her arm around an imaginary husband by extending her arm on the back of a chair or seat next to her.

(Site Expansion) She will move her purse over a little to indicate the vacant seat is taken, hoping that the host will pick up on the fact that her husband is about to arrive.

(Turn and Fake) She will turn sideways on the seat bench and pull her knee up so as to take up the space next to her. This is sometimes accompanied by removing her shoe to create the impression that she has an injury and couldn't possibly dance.

(Deflection) She will engage the waitress or waiter in an animated and very serious conversation.

(Head Down) The lady will stare intently at a program or any piece of paper with her head overly bowed, yet sneak a peek to see who is approaching.

It matters not what method they use; it normally works. Hosts do not, under any circumstances, want these abandoned seat savers to feel uncomfortable. I have learned to recognize the signs and bypass these women. I do not want an upset husband to come charging out of nowhere to save the same wife he had neglected previously. I have had a couple of reminders about how unpleasant that can be.

DANCE WITH ME...DANCE WITH ME

J ust as there are ladies who don't care to dance, and let us know it, there are ladies who do want to dance and try to let us know it. These messages can be verbal or non-verbal. The surefire way for a lady to secure a dance is to ask. No host I have known would turn down a lady. Of course, that is often regarded as too forward by ladies of my generation. Thus they resort to more subtle but nevertheless effective ways of making their wishes known. Among those that are easily identifiable, with my code, are:

(Down In Front) Sitting by herself or with other like-minded ladies in front of the lounges and showrooms. This certainly enhances one's chances of being invited to dance since that puts the lady right where the dancing is. This is most ladies' favorite.

(Tap Time) Tapping one's foot on the floor or fingers on the table in time to the music. If accompanied by eye contact and a smile, it is a sure winner.

(Front Ending) Showing up without a partner at daytime dance classes. This assures that we hosts become aware that she dances and is available at the evening's sets.

(John Alden Move) Enlisting the help of a server or friend to approach a host on her behalf to state that she wishes to dance and doesn't want to be overlooked. This always works, too.

Whatever the lady's approach, at least one host will pick up on it very early in the cruise. Once the lady has had one dance, she can then relax. All hosts will quickly notice or be informed in one fashion or another, and she will be included in the dancing whenever she shows up. In my twenty-three years of hosting, I have logged 175 cruises. Each of those cruises averaged about twelve days. On any particular day, I typically dance five sets of thirteen songs each. That equates to about 120,000 dances.

PERSISTENCE

The ship pulled into Mumbai, India, and fellow host Richard and I went ashore. He was interested in going to the famous Crawford Market, officially named the Mahatma Phule Market. He thought it was about eight blocks away. We sought some specific directions when we got off the ship and were directed with a wave of the hand. We were on our way.

First, we had about a two hundred-yard walk to the exit gate of the port. Immediately outside the gate, taxi drivers surrounded us, wanting to be of assistance. We declined, knowing we had only a short walk to the market. One particular driver got in his cab and began to follow us. At each intersection, he would ask if we wanted a cab. His wide grin was designed to wear us down. But we declined. After about eight blocks (and as many inquiries from this still-smiling cabbie), we asked a bystander how much farther it was to the market. "Not far, that way," was the response, and off we trudged again. The cabbie still followed us. We walked maybe twelve blocks. Still no market, but our ever-present cabbie was right with us.

I was beginning to believe we were hopelessly lost and maybe the taxi was not a bad idea, but Richard insisted on continuing our trek. Fifteen minutes later and I don't know how many blocks, we finally saw the intended destination. We must have walked nearly two miles to get to this "very close" market.

As we entered, our persistent cabbie drove off. We toured the market for about an hour purchasing some must-have trinkets for friends and family. When we exited, there he was again. Now the cabbie asked if we needed a taxi back to the ship. Richard and I looked at each other, shook our heads, and climbed in. But before leaving, we asked the price of the return trip. This is standard procedure most everywhere in the world where taxis are not metered. His answer was two dollars. It goes without saying that Richard and I tipped him generously.

An Hour Well Spent

The Mississippi riverboat I was assigned to as a dance host was docked in Prairie du Chien, Wisconsin, in July 1991. It was about 10:00 a.m. and passengers had disembarked, with the new crowd not scheduled to board until about 4:00 p.m. I was standing at the railing considering a walk into town. I had never been to Wisconsin before, so I was looking forward to that. As I walked down the gangway, I spotted a couple with a young girl standing on the levee. They were admiring this impressive riverboat and were taking pictures of each other with it in the background.

I approached them, introduced myself, as did they, and asked if they would like a picture of the three of them in front of the riverboat. With smiles, Lynn and Sharon said yes, and I snapped off three or four shots of them and their twelve-year-old daughter, Kimberly. As we chatted, I learned that they owned a farm about eighty miles to the west in Iowa and had taken time away from

their chores just to come to see the riverboat and do a little camp-
ing. As we talked I learned more about their farm and their daughter Kimberly's involvement in her local 4H club.

On a hunch, I asked if they could wait a few minutes while I
went back aboard. I found the first mate and explained to him that
I had three guests I would like to bring aboard. He agreed, and I
bounded down the gangway to my new acquaintances. I told them
they could take a short tour if they had time. With expressions
of surprise and slight hesitation on their part, I ushered them
aboard. I showed them some of the cabins, the galley, the dining
room, the showroom, and the lounge. Kimberly was wide-eyed as
she oohed and aahed at opulence I guessed neither she nor her
parents had ever witnessed before. I took them to the wheelhouse
and took a picture of the three of them holding on to the six-foot-
round wooden steering wheel. As they left they seemed happy and
maybe a little overwhelmed. They all thanked me, and Lynn said
that never in their wildest dreams did they think they would get to
come aboard. These fine hard-working folks from America's heart-
land had viewed firsthand a piece of Americana not many people
get to see, and I felt really good I had made it possible.

TRANSCENDING CULTURES

Ifirst met Toshiko on a cruise departing from San Juan, Puerto Rico, and heading through the Caribbean, Panama Canal, and along the Mexican Riviera. This lady was one of twenty Japanese guests on an upscale cruise to Los Angeles.

It was apparent from the start that the group was led by a distinguished gentleman; I'll call him Mr. Osaki. He was held in reverence and shown great respect by the others. It was with some trepidation that I found myself escorting this whole group as we toured Tortola, British West Indies, in an open-air safari-type bus. Besides me, only Mr. Osaki and the group translator spoke English, so I was sure this tour would be a linguistic disaster. I soon caught everyone's contagious anticipation and eagerness to get going. At the first stop on the tour, I offered via semi-sign language, that I would be happy to take photographs. Thereafter, on every stop, I had the privilege of taking an ever-increasing number of photos with an ever-increasing number of cameras. I also learned that most members of the group were learning English and relished practicing with me.

The farther we traveled around the island, the more animated and happy my Japanese charges became. Everything they saw was spectacular, and what I feared would be a reserved group became delightful "children." By the end of the tour, I had made some wonderful new friends. The smiles and bows I received as I made my final count to make sure we left no one behind filled me with joy that I had seldom experienced.

As I entered one of the lounges where dancing was scheduled that evening, Mr. Osaki greeted me and pointed to each of the ladies he would like me to dance with. Although that is a little unorthodox, he was a paying passenger and seemed to carry a lot of clout, so I went along with his requests. I danced with very few American ladies that evening. I passed on the word to the other hosts, and all of the Japanese ladies got plenty of dancing for the rest of the cruise. Among the ladies I danced with was Toshika, a very beautiful lady in her late forties. She was tall, slender, and had an infectious smile. Her choices of attire were impeccable, and she carried herself with quiet dignity. In very halting English, she asked if I danced international or American style. I replied American, since I was only briefly introduced to international style dancing and would never willingly initiate it. It soon became obvious that this lady was an excellent dancer, and I enjoyed my several dances with her. The waltz was her favorite dance. She was like a feather as she glided through every step I knew and then smiled and slightly bowed to me at the end of each dance.

It was not an accident that I danced several times with Toshika on the last evening of the cruise. I had found a soft spot in my heart for Mr. Osaki and his entire group. Of course I had a special place for this lady. I bid everyone farewell and chalked up knowing them all as a big plus for me. I assumed that would be the last time I saw any of them.

About one year later, when I was a dance host on another ship of the same cruise line, I bumped into Mr. Osaki. This time he and his group were touring the Mediterranean Sea. He smiled and said hello, and we chatted. Later that evening when I entered the lounge, I was struck with déjà vu. Mr. Osaki stood up, waved, smiled, and once again pointed to the ladies he wished me to dance with. As before, I danced with each one and advised the other hosts to do the same. I was thrilled to see that among the ladies was my friend Toshika. As always, she was a wonderful dance partner and prevailed upon me to have our picture taken together by the ever-present photographer.

On the last night of this cruise, Toshika and I presented each other with a copy of that photograph. We both laughed, and I noticed that the reverse side of the photo had her full name and address. I had given her one of my personal cards. I made sure I got to dance the last dance of the last night with Toshika. As we finished we turned to each other, and once again I felt I probably would never see this new friend again. I did notice the glistening of her eyes and a tiny tear coming down her cheek, even though she turned to try to hide it. It might be my ego, but I believe that I had become as special a person to her as she had to me. I sure hope I get to see this Japanese beauty again sometime.

Pumping Water

As a reasonably accomplished dancer, I am always on the lookout for new steps or routines to add to my repertoire. Of course, the dance classes aboard ships are great places to learn new steps, as are the ones I attend when I'm home. Watching other accomplished gentleman as they dance is another option.

The evening aboard ship when the captain's formal party is held is one time when it's better to shut your eyes, though. This is when the guest couples show up in all their finery to meet the staff and socialize with their fellow passengers. We hosts are also there to supply dancing partners for the unescorted ladies or wives of gentlemen who choose not to dance. These events are the few times when gentlemen who do not dance, except under duress or fear of consequences, will be on the floor with their wives. Somewhere in the depths of these men's minds they have the false impression that "more is better." They are all over the floor unaware of, or not caring about, dance etiquette. They pump their left arm along with the ladies' right as though they were pumping water. Exaggerated movements of all body parts signify a high level of dance knowledge in their minds. On such nights I make sure I keep near the edge of the floor and out of harm's way.

I've witnessed ripped gowns, lost shoes, split tux pants, popped shirt studs, and more, due to over-enthusiastic men who want to make sure everyone in the room knows they can dance. In my earlier days, I was one of them. But I eventually learned that the gentleman's role in dancing is to make the lady look good, and downplaying his movements is one of the key ways to ensure that goal is met. My hat goes off to the ladies these gentlemen dance with and also those gentlemen who later asked us hosts to dance with their wives.

FALLING OVER YOU

B eing a complete gentleman is a cardinal rule of dance hosting. Many hosts are terrific dancers, and it is not unusual to find among us those who are dance instructors ashore. But many of the ladies we dance with are novices. Nonetheless, from time to time, a host feels it necessary to display his talents on the dance floor for all to admire, and that causes a problem. Mason was one of these overzealous hosts.

One particular evening, Mason was with a lady who was not the best of dancers, but he zipped around the floor as if he had a real pro in his arms. I knew something was going to happen, but there was no way I could stop it. About halfway through the dance, Mason tried to perform a very intricate step, and the lady fell. In his efforts to prevent this, Mason lost his balance, and the two of them sprawled on the floor. He hopped up and gave the old "it wasn't my fault" pose and shaking his head as though somehow the floor was to fault. Of course, others stopped dancing to assist the lady to her feet. She had sprained her ankle, and unfortunately that was the last we saw of her for the rest of the cruise. This showoff behavior had cost a lady guest her full cruise experience.

Over the years, I have seen several other hosts show the same disrespect for dance etiquette and violate common sense rules by dropping ladies. My philosophy is simple, and I recommend it to anyone who will listen. I determine quickly what level of dance my partner is capable of, and that's how we dance. It only takes me about three steps to make this decision. On subsequent dances with the same partner, I may throw in some new simple variation until she is comfortable with that and then move on.

Rarely do I over judge the ability of a lady who is not a very accomplished dancer. On the other hand, I recently under judged the dancing style of a very bouncy and energetic fifty-something bundle of unbridled energy who appeared to be a quite accomplished dancer. I observed, as one of my fellow hosts danced with her, that she danced well, though all her moves tended to be incredibly exaggerated. As the last dance of the first set was announced, I invited Serena to dance, and the number being played was a nice quiet rumba. The quietness I intended was quickly interrupted by her exaggerated hip movements and body positioning as I tried unsuccessfully to lead or at least guide her through the dance. After all, the gentleman is supposed to lead and the lady follow. I finally got what I thought was a semblance of control as the dance was ending. We were near the edge of the dance floor, and she spotted a friend of hers standing there, and as the dance ended she abruptly executed a huge backward dip presumably to impress someone. Unfortunately, I was caught unaware and could not prevent her from going to the floor, dragging me with her. I scurried to my feet, helped her to hers, and asked if she was okay. She and the nearby people were more concerned about whether I was injured, and I assured them I was not.

I felt, then saw, blood oozing down the cuff on the right sleeve of my tux shirt. I hurried to my cabin to inspect the damage, but not before a couple of people witnessed this aftermath of my tumble. I had braced my fall with my right forearm, and the cuff link of my tux shirt had left me with a small cut on my wrist. It looked much worse than it really was. I cleansed the little wound, applied a Band-Aid, and donned a clean tux shirt and dismissed the incident as a lesson learned.

Later that evening my "fall" became the talk of the dancing venue since Georgina, a lady who was a frequent passenger with the cruise line, decided to relate my little accident with anyone who would listen. Unfortunately, every time she retold the story my condition grew worse to the point where later in the evening one guest suggested I retire for the night and tend to my wounds. His understanding, based on his received information, prompted him to suggest I have an X-ray taken to see what bone(s) I had broken when I had suddenly "collapsed." There was no mention of my dancing partner or her unorthodox dancing. I learned later that Georgina, who was passing on the detailed description of the incident, had not even witnessed it.

The next day, no less than three guests and one staff member approached me to check on my condition. Since a ship is like a little town, I was sure I had not heard the end of my encounter with the floor. Serena sought me out late that evening, and with an overly exaggerated flourish of attention for all to see, heaped unasked for and unwanted hugs upon me showing concern for my health. She asked what the ship's doctor had said and what treatment I was following up with.

Count On Us

Every once in a while on a cruise the unescorted ladies get into the counting game. It normally occurs when we hosts are overwhelmingly outnumbered by the ladies desiring to dance. It goes something like this: We try hard to make sure all of the ladies get an equal chance. But occasionally, one lady will sit out more dances than she thinks is appropriate. Then the counting begins.

"That woman has danced three times, and I only danced once," Georgia will say, while Natalie points out, "You guys haven't danced with me for four dances." The other ladies plug into this mentality, and soon they are all counting dances. It is a scene out of a high school sock hop, and there's no way the dance hosts can win.

If this continues, one of the "girls" will surely seek out the cruise director with her complaint. When that happens, he has no choice but to take action. Normally this involves the dance instruction team or some other staffer showing up at each dance session and counting the dances as well. They, in turn, report back to the cruise director. Then a little meeting is called with the hosts to make us aware of what we already know. If the complaining lady's name is mentioned, that in itself upgrades her chances of getting more dances, for we hosts do not want to appear to be playing favorites.

One particularly clever lady named Alice actually had a mechanical counter and figured out that she was getting an average of two dances per set. (A typical dance set has twelve or thirteen arrangements.) Alice would arrive early, take a seat with one of the hosts, and engage him in conversation. When the music started, he of course, would ask her to dance. After that, she would wait her turn—maybe six dances—get a second dance and then leave. She would go to the casino or the piano bar and then return before the beginning of the next set, using the same strategy again.

Another delightful lady, Judy, from Miami, would try to enhance her chances of getting extra dances by offering to buy beverages for the hosts in the hopes they would pay attention to her. Invitations to lunch, dinner, or any other function by one of our dancing ladies also can become suspect, especially if the conversations drift to dancing or the number of ladies aboard the ship. We hosts are always aware of the number of ladies who wish to dance and who have not had a chance as yet. My rule of thumb is to select for my next partner a lady who is sitting. On a very crowded dance floor, it is difficult to ensure that all ladies get exactly the same number of dances. All hosts will agree that the ladies can count on us to do the very best and not play favorites. We know what constant complaints from a lady can lead to!

TRILOGY

As hosts we need to be ever mindful that, on occasions, single male passengers will show up to dance with the ladies. As good hosts, we make sure these paying guests get first dibs, so to speak, on choosing dancing partners. This can be a good thing or a bad thing depending on the situation. Here are three examples of just such men I have met at our dance venues:

The Good

The evening was going smoothly. We six hosts had about fifteen ladies to dance with, and everyone seemed to be having fun. I looked up from the dance floor to see a gentleman guest standing just inside the door assessing the situation. He was obviously trying to make up his mind whether he should brave this or not. Whether we like it or not, hosts intimidate most men when it comes to dancing. Compared to us, they feel they are not good enough, and they don't want to appear foolish. I approached this gentleman, introduced myself as a host, and asked if he was going to join in the fun. He said his name was Felix and his home was Fort Lauderdale, Florida. He was a good-looking older guy with a pleasant smile, and I knew instinctively he would be a hit with the ladies. He offered that he was not a very good dancer and didn't know if he would fit in. I assured him he would, and introduced him to the nearest lady.

He did all right on the first dance. At the end of the set, I introduced him to the other hosts and several other ladies. He danced for the rest of the evening, and none of the ladies seemed to notice or care about his lack of dancing skills. I said good-night and that I hoped he would join us the next evening. When a male guest fits in with the dancing crowd, it is great for us hosts. In effect, we have an additional guy to help. This makes for more dances for the ladies as well.

Felix joined us each night for a while and even started showing up at the daily dance classes. Each night he seemed to be more at ease and confided to me that he was having a ball. But one evening I noticed he wasn't there and neither was one of the ladies who always danced with us. The same thing happened the next night. Eventually I ran into Felix and told him we missed him. He said that he and one of the dancing ladies had found each other and, if they came back to the evening dancing, it would be as a couple. Since we do not dance with escorted ladies unless we are specifically asked by the gentleman, I assured him that the lady in question was his wife as far as we hosts were concerned, and we would not be asking her to dance. They showed up that evening and danced the night away.

The Bad

Once in a while, we have a host who errs in his judgment or misunderstands a situation, and we hope it doesn't cause a bigger problem. On this particular occasion, one of my fellow hosts, Lester, approached a table next to the dance floor where a gentleman guest was casually conversing with three ladies we had previously danced with. He asked one to dance. The gentleman in question, Sydney, took exception. He said he planned to have that dance but didn't indicate which lady he intended to ask. Lester extended his hand, which one of the ladies accepted, and he led her to the floor. He hadn't done anything wrong, but he probably should have held back to be sure what Sydney's intentions were. After the dance, Sydney got in Lester's face and got nasty. Then at the end of the dance set, he stormed toward where we eight hosts were sitting and got right in my face. I listened, apologized, and assured him we would be mindful of his concerns. I then asked why he came to me since I wasn't the one who had committed the presumed faux pas. He replied, "Well, I know you, and you run this show, so I want *you* to take care of it." (I might add that it was evident by this point that Sydney had been over-served at the adjacent bar.) I assured him that there was no lead host, and I certainly was not the spokesperson for this group. Nevertheless, I also assured him that this situation would not come up again. Privately, we all agreed to be careful of Sydney, and some of the hosts said they would not go near him, which wasn't right either. The next morning I saw Sydney on deck having a cup of coffee. I asked him if I could join him, and he invited me to sit down. I explained that I had chatted more with the guys about his concerns. He was more mellow and thanked me but added that he was going to be on the ship for fifty more days and that at the end of each cruise he would be grading the hosts as all passengers do on their evaluation form. His message was clear. He considered this ship "his turf."

The Ugly

My good friend Ed, two other hosts, and I were engaged in our nightly dance routines aboard a ship with a posh dancing venue that was packed with couples, single ladies, two single men, and our dance instructor team. To make this evening even more special, there were four ladies in the room whom we knew very well from previous cruises. The two who Ed and I knew best were sitting at a table near the floor and were busy dancing and socializing. I noticed that one of the nearby single guys was eyeing these two ladies, Lee Ann and Jane. His attention did not go unnoticed, and at break they asked Ed and me to sit with them. Lee Ann told Ed, "I don't like the look of that guy who has been eyeing us. If you see him about to ask me to dance, please intercede." We delicately suggested that perhaps they could just say no if asked to dance, and they agreed to do that.

We give gentleman passengers first choice for ladies to dance with, but we can't wait too long. By the time a guy has processed in his mind the music being played, whether he can dance to it, whom to ask to dance, and then ask her, we hosts have chosen a lady and are on the floor. Plus, in this case, our bosses, (the dance instructors) were eyeballing us to make sure we were doing our job.

So sure enough, this guy asks Jane to dance, and she politely declines. He retreats, unhappily. About two dances later, he started for the table again, but this time ever-alert Ed got there first and invited Lee Ann to dance. As they passed the guest on the way to the floor, he stepped in front of Ed, gave him a forceful forearm shiver and announced this was his dance. Ed brushed him aside, and he and Lee Ann took the floor. The livid gentleman sought out the dance instructors, had words with them, and then took off.

At the end of the evening, the dance instructors asked us hosts to remain behind for a little meeting. They said that the gentleman had told them of Ed's behavior, and he was unhappy. The lady member of the dance instructor team told Ed he had to track down the guy and apologize. I asked if they had seen what transpired, and they said they had not. This guy had told them that Ed had pushed him out of the way so he could dance with his "girlfriend." I told them that that wasn't what happened at all, and Ed did not owe him an apology for protecting Lee Ann from unwanted advances, let alone for being physically abused. Nevertheless, they insisted. Ed gave it a lot of thought, but he elected not to extend an apology. It takes just one situation like that to ruin everyone's cruise.

MEE AND JEEM

The Chinese take great pride in their children and grandchildren. Many youngsters take music and singing lessons after school, and it was at one of these programs that I found myself with a group of thirty or so cruise-line passengers. I was escorting a tour to a children's music program in Xian, China. While waiting for the group to reassemble after some free time, I noticed a Chinese lady with a very cute nine-year-old girl at her side. The little girl was dressed in a school-type, spotless blue jumper with a white, long sleeved blouse, white knee socks, and black patent leather shoes. Her black pigtails with red ribbons bracketed her shiny face. The lady, I guessed, was the child's grandmother. As I sat on a bench, they both approached me slowly. I smiled and nodded, and they came closer. My heart was already beginning to melt. With a little shove, the grandmother urged the youngster forward. In a clear, but halting, voice she said, "Mee," as she pointed to herself. I repeated her name and smiled. She smiled, and the grandmother smiled. I then pointed to myself and said "Jim." Mee pointed to me and said, "Jeem." Again smiles all around. Then Mee pointed and said, "American?" I nodded. Now the smiles were even wider. It became obvious that the grandmother wanted her granddaughter to have an encounter with someone from a Western civilization.

Two of the ladies in my group showed up about that time, and I introduced them to my new friend, Mee. One of them wanted to offer Mee a handkerchief and was thoughtful enough ask me first. I gestured to the grandmother whether it would be okay for Mee to accept this little gift. She nodded her consent. With a blush, Mee joyfully accepted the hankie and placed it in her blouse pocket. By that time more of my group had assembled and were boarding our bus. I bowed and said, "Good-bye, Mee." With a curtsey, she replied, "Good-bye Jeem." I looked at the grandmother and bowed slightly, but before I could say anything she said in perfect English, "Thank you so much for your kindness to my granddaughter."

EUREKA!

July 22, 1997 found me in Juneau, Alaska, as a dance host aboard an upscale cruise ship. My assignment for the day was to be an escort for a gold-panning and salmon-bake tour. The day was overcast with a little drizzle, and my group of seventeen adults and two pre-teens was not all that excited as we tendered from our ship to the port.

Standing next to our small bus was Dave, our driver, guide, and prospector for the day. He was a burly guy in his early forties with a neat beard and typical lumberjack clothing. With a warm smile and booming welcome, he handed each of us a little packet that contained a plastic hooded poncho. As he began the tour of Juneau, I noticed the mood of my brood had lightened a bit. As he drove, Dave pointed out the sights of Alaska's capital and told stories about the early days and the characters that dared come here to seek their fortunes. His narratives were loaded with funny stories, and soon the giggles turned into laughter as we arrived at our gold-panning destination, about seven miles from the city.

As the drizzle continued, he guided us down a muddy path for about three hundred feet to a clearing next to a small stream. He gathered us around a square table that held a number of green plastic pans, a five-gallon bucket filled with riverbed soil, and other gold-panning paraphernalia. Dave showed the group how to swirl the soil in a pan with water from the stream. After a minute or so, we marveled at the little flecks of gold that appeared in the remaining water. With an eyedropper he carefully siphoned the gold-speckled water and deposited it into a little plastic vial. He promised that before we left, each of us would have some gold to take home. It was as if the rain had never existed. I could feel an electricity of anticipation coming from this group of panhandlers. Gold fever, I thought.

Everyone got down on their haunches at the stream and began to practice the art of panning for gold. Some did well, others not so, but Dave kept repeating in a loud voice, "Stay with the pan." He helped the two youngsters with their efforts and continued to shout, "Stay with the pan" to all. True to his word, Dave made sure everybody, even I, had a little vial of water with traces of gold to take home. A check of my watch told me we should get on with the tour, but it was difficult to get the group to depart. Finally, with Dave in the lead, we retraced our steps up the now muddier path to the bus. The continuing drizzle did not dampen the spirits of the group, and they bragged to one another about their adventure. Dave continued telling gold stories, so the fifteen-minute ride to the salmon bake site went quickly.

We sat at picnic tables and devoured our sumptuous lunch of grilled salmon, potato salad, coleslaw, and baked beans. Dave and I made sure that the wine jugs on each table were never empty, and we had soft drinks for the kids. After the strawberry shortcake dessert, we boarded our bus for the return to dockside. I started out with seventeen adults and two youngsters, and I returned with nineteen "kids." Dave smiled as he shook everyone's hand as they got off the bus. I gathered the group and whispered a little secret message to them. As Dave readied to leave, we all turned and in unison said, "Stay with the pan," and applauded. His smile was priceless. I noticed the drizzle had stopped. I looked to see if I could see a rainbow, but no such luck. I guess we were lucky enough for one day. We had experienced firsthand some of what the original prospectors must have felt.

KEEP YOUR MOUTH SHUT

We hosts enjoy some really fabulous benefits as part of our relationship with cruise lines. Though we aren't paid, we do get transportation to and from our assignments, passenger-quality cabins, and all meals. On our free time, we can volunteer to escort land tours at no cost. At sea, we can avail ourselves of most of the amenities that the paying passengers can, including the lectures and shows, when we are not on duty. Another perk that we sometimes get is a beverage allowance, so we can treat guests to a drink from time to time. This comes in especially handy when we are hosting a dining table, allowing us to treat everyone on behalf of the cruise line when we deem it appropriate. It has never been clear to me what perks, if any, other members of the entertainment staff receive. That being the case, I never talk about my deal around any of them, and most certainly not to passengers.

In August 1994, on a ten-day big-band cruise from Miami to Lisbon, Portugal, it was particularly embarrassing when one of my dance host colleagues, Dexter, new to this cruise line, was sharing information about host business that was really private. I can only assume he was trying to ingratiate himself to the passengers, or maybe he was just bragging.

The third night of the cruise, when I arrived at the dining table I was hosting, a surprise greeted me. I had hardly seated myself when one of the ladies, Jessica, chimed in with, "Well, Dexter told me you hosts have a beverage allowance, so you can buy the drinks for the table tonight." While I cringed inside, I said, "Of course, it would be my pleasure." Later that evening at the dancing venue, Jessica announced what Dexter had told her to those in attendance, so naturally they expected one or more of us six hosts to do the honors for beverages. Dexter smiled as he nodded his assent. My good buddy, Jason, a very experienced host from the Napa Valley, didn't miss a beat when he told the group he was sure Dexter could handle this little amenity. Up to this point, a glass of water with lemon had been their drink of choice.

I feel it is up to me to determine when, where, and with whom I choose to host cocktails or wine. I certainly would not expect to be maneuvered into a position where I felt it necessary to do so. Obviously, Jason felt the same way. He and I arranged a meeting with the other hosts so we could explain why it was not a good idea to broadcast our business. I told them about an experience with my father many years earlier when he told me that if you have a good thing going that others might not have, then it's better to keep your mouth shut. All the hosts but one (guess who?) agreed that keeping quiet about our perks and our arrangements with the cruise line was a good idea.

What's In A Name?

All of the cruise lines that value their dance host program have concluded they can use this captured resource for non-dancing purposes. As part of the contract we sign, it is suggested that the host be a person spreading good will among all passengers. Providing directions to confused guests becomes a routine duty. Hosting a table for dining also provides an opportunity for us to add our own personal upbeat touch to the passengers' cruising experience. Additionally, hosts are given the opportunity to escort land tours when the ships are in port. This gives the tour managers an extra set of hands and eyes to help assist passengers and spread good will with the locals.

In an effort to make this as easy as possible for all, the hosts are provided with and must wear name badges. This identifies them as part of the ship's staff and is a welcome sign to newly embarked passengers with questions. It also makes it easy for the name tag wearer to approach a guest and welcome them aboard. For dance hosts it provides an opportunity to approach ladies who appear to be unattached and make them aware of the dance program. This works well, and it helps assure that they don't find out about the program as they are ready to leave the ship.

Late in July 1998, aboard a cruise ship sailing from New York to Montreal, I stationed myself near the ship's lobby and offered a "welcome aboard" to embarking passengers. One lady, who I judged to be traveling alone, boarded, and I welcomed her with my pitch for the dance program. She tightened up and mumbled something as she scurried off toward the elevator. Undaunted, I continued my little deal and saw two ladies who were together. I welcomed them, said my name was Jim, and added I hoped I would see them for dancing this evening. They both recoiled and turned away. I headed for my cabin to check that I didn't have food in my teeth or my fly wasn't unzipped when I noticed I had forgotten to put my name badge on.

I had lost my identity, so to speak, and I was no longer recognized as part of the welcoming committee. I learned never to forget to wear my name badge unless, of course, I was on my own in port. Even then, I have found that in most countries wearing it is usually worth some kind of discount at the stores and with street vendors, and a great item to be wearing to ward off persistent peddlers.

THE OLD SWITCHEROO!

I was escorting a group of cruise-line passengers through Istanbul, Turkey. We had toured the Blue Mosque, the Spice Market, the opulent Topkapi Palace, and the ever-present carpet factories. Next stop was the Grand Bazaar. It was here that we had cut the troops loose to shop. As they explored the maze of streets in this huge market, I went in search of Christmas gifts. I have found that if I'm diligent, I can finish most of my Christmas shopping each year during my travels. I spotted a vendor selling beautiful skewers. They would make a good gift for my one son whose middle name is "barbeque." The bearded Turk extolled the attributes of these shiny stainless-steel skewers, and we began the negotiating. He wanted five US dollars each. They really were beautiful and, after much haggling, I got a price of ten US dollars for four. I was satisfied. The Turk had a quiver of these skewers slung across his shoulder, and he deftly extracted three with his right hand as he held the one I had negotiated for in his left.

Quicker than the eye could follow, he wrapped the four skewers in a newspaper and was about to put them in a plastic bag when I asked to see them again. There, next to the one beautiful stainless-steel skewer, were three cheap aluminum ones. I looked at him disappointedly as I walked off. My son would have to wait for his skewers until another time.

Seasoned by this experience, it was a little easier to spot a ploy on another trip. This time it was in Kenya, outside a game preserve we had just visited. I watched a chatty nice-looking young man with a big smile wrap the small carved wooden elephant I had just purchased for six dollars. I was sure my granddaughter, Samantha, would love it. He deftly slid the beautiful elephant beneath his display counter and made a great ceremony of wrapping my prize with brightly colored paper. As I was about to hand him the money, my antenna went up. He was just too glib. I asked to look at the elephant again. His smile and chatter ceased as he slowly unwrapped it. Somehow the elephant I had almost purchased now had two broken tusks. I walked to another salesman nearby and made my purchase, making sure the young hustler saw me.

EEZY PEEZY

One of the more interesting things that have occurred to me in my career as a dance host has nothing to do with my duties at sea or the people I met on my assignments. It is with the guys I know back home. Many times over the years, male friends have approached me about what I do on the cruise ships. Invariably they say, "Hey that sounds easy, I can do that." To which I always reply, "Then you should." If they ask, I advise them to put together a dance DVD and submit it with an application to the cruise lines. Simply go online and seek out opportunities just as you would with any other job search. Some ask me to front for them as a reference. I am not about to put my hard-earned reputation with the cruise lines on the line just because they're acquaintances or friends. I do supply some more information that can give them an edge. For instance, I tell them most cruise lines have strict dress codes for hosts including a tuxedo, white dinner jacket, blue blazer, and an assortment of upscale attire. They must be willing to invest in their wardrobe if they're to be accepted. I add that there is no pay, but rather it's an exchange of services.

I explain that most cruise lines use agents to secure their dance hosts. Agents charge for placing people on the ships, and their rate is around twenty-five to thirty dollars per day. Since a host's commitment is normally around thirty days, that means an outlay of seven hundred fifty to nine hundred dollars. Some cruise lines may require hosts to pay for transportation to and from the ship. This can be significant if ports of embarkation and debarkation are overseas. Only about 10 percent of the guys are still interested after hearing all this. To these few I give the telephone number, address, and e-mail of several of the agents I know and remind them I'm just supplying information, not acting as a referral. Over the years, only three gentlemen actually followed through, and all three got placements through an agent to become a dance host. Of those three, one reported back after just one cruise, and said it just wasn't for him. Another told me that the agent had said he did not quite fit what the cruise line was looking for, and he was not invited back. The third has had a successful career as a dance host, and acted in that capacity for about ten years. I don't see him often, but when I do he never fails to thank me for helping him get started. He is one of the lucky ones to join a group of about two hundred gentlemen worldwide who sail the high seas as dance hosts.

REBA

R eba was a strikingly beautiful brunette from Mississippi. She dressed very attractively and carried herself with great poise. This former schoolteacher, whose husband had died in an auto accident many years ago, was a frequent cruiser, I was told. Though well known by fellow passengers and staff, she spent a lot of time by herself during the days, but never failed to show up at the nightly dance venues.

At a meeting early in the cruise, our dance instructor team had advised us that Reba liked to dance by herself, and that we should be mindful of that. I didn't take that to mean we should not at least ask her to dance, even if she refused. Sure enough, the first evening Reba danced to some really torchy music by herself. She swung and swayed in her filmy dress attire. It swirled as she pirouetted, and she seemed off in another world. At the second set of the evening, I spotted Reba sitting at her table alone and approached her. I asked if she would care to dance, and she smiled and said yes. We negotiated a waltz flawlessly. She was as light as a feather and responded gracefully to any lead I made. As I escorted her back to her seat, I made a mental note to ask her for a dance again later.

At the next break, one of the dance hosts reminded me that we were not to ask Reba to dance. To make sure I knew what was expected of me, I asked the lady part of the dance instructor team if that was her intent when they told us about Reba's habit of dancing by herself. She said that no one but me had ever asked Reba to dance before because they thought she preferred to dance by herself. An astute lady passenger seated near where we were talking overheard our conversation, leaned in, and offered, "I don't think she is dancing by herself."

I was so taken by Reba that I wrote this little poem.
It may seem odd at first glance
To watch this solo lady dance
But to her it's a guy in her arms
She basks in memory of his charm
Would that we might have her chance

WHEW!

Shanghai has got to be one of fastest-growing cities in the Far East. It was certainly much larger in 2004 than the first time I visited ten years earlier. On the evening before we were to dock there, a fellow dance host, Marvin, and I were musing about what to do on our day in port. Marvin suggested we go from the Bund across the Huangpu River, and explore the Oriental Pearl TV Tower. It is a new tall building with a unique structural tripod base. Sitting atop the tripod is a huge globe-shaped portion that contains offices, restaurants, and TV studios. Above this is a circular shaft that supports yet another smaller globe containing more restaurants, offices, and an observation deck. Above this is the mast of the building with antennae for radio and TV transmission. It is an engineering marvel and a popular tourist attraction. Maryanne and Herman, who were guests on the ship, were also planning to visit the "Pearl" and asked if they could go with us. We arranged an early meeting time in the lobby.

Next morning, Marvin and I arrived, as did Herman. He said his wife had second thoughts about going to the Pearl, so they were opting out. She was hesitant to do the ferry ride and the walking, he said. I told him he was welcome to go with us. He hesitated, then shrugged and said he would pass also. I knew he wanted to join us, but I guess he sensed the "price" would be too high for him.

Marvin and I disembarked and got directions to the passenger ferry to cross the Huangpu River. Soon we are in the midst of a swarm of Chinese also heading for the ferry. There were no other Caucasians in the group, so we instinctively held onto our cameras a little tighter and glanced around a lot. We didn't have to worry about missing the ferry because we were swept forward with no chance of escape had we wanted to. As I was about to pay my fare, I felt an elbow in my rib cage. I looked to my left as a tiny lady pushed me aside and thrust down her fare. Eventually, Marvin and I boarded and found a place aft so we could avoid disembowelment on our exit. At this point, we were sort of happy that Maryanne and Herman were not with us.

We got off the ferry, and with the Pearl in sight, strode off toward it. The streets were not as crowded, and soon we spotted three strapping young Chinese lads coming our way. At my urging, we crossed to the other side of the street only to see the trio do likewise. We walked on, clutching our valuables ever tighter. When they were about five feet from us one of them said, "Good morning, Mr. American." The three of them smiled and giggled, and Marvin and I relaxed and replied in unison, "Good morning."

Onward we walked, and within five minutes we were at the Pearl. The line to enter was very long and almost entirely made up of Chinese school children. We took our place in line and were again pushed forward to the ticket booth. This time, though, there was no dig to the ribs, but two young boys actually stepped aside so we could buy our tickets. We thanked them, they nodded, bowed slightly, and we entered the next line for the elevators. Eventually we got to the observation level, and the view was spectacular. We could see up and down the river and across to the Bund. We took some pictures of the children, with their permission of course, and then spent about ten minutes as they took pictures of us and their classmates. Around noon we retraced our steps to the ferry. It was not nearly as crowded. We spent the rest of our day exploring the length of the Bund, and as we were boarding the ship we agreed that the day was well spent, and in retrospect wished that Maryanne and Herman had indeed joined us. They too would have experienced the un-comfortableness of a crowd, the inquisitiveness of three teenagers, and the polite behavior of young school children. Just like at home!

RUMP ROAST

Diane and her mother, Joyce, were having a fabulous cruise in the Mediterranean. I first met them when escorting a land tour in Malta. They were lively and animated and seemed to find something worthwhile in everything they saw and every place we visited. They were nearly carbon copies of one another. Both were short, a little chubby, and had the carrot-colored hair and the cherub face that only the Irish can claim. They were early risers, as I am, so I joined them for coffee most mornings and got to know them pretty well.

One morning in Tunis, they mentioned that they were looking forward to their land tour that day. I said that perhaps we would be on the same bus again and I would accompany them. As it turned out they were not in my group but the one right before me. I got a chance to observe the following exchange between one of America's best and her newfound admirer.

The salesmen of Tunis are relentless. They follow the passengers forever trying to sell their wares. "One dollar," was the cry of the day. The old come-on worked sometimes, but more often than not, it was ignored. Diane and her mother were no exception as they were pestered ad infinitum. One young huckster tagged along with his "one dollar" pitch and was rebuffed repeatedly by Diane. Finally out of desperation, or a change of game plan, the young pitchman reached out and stroked Diane's backside.

Diane spun around, shoved her nose in his face, and shouted, "That will be one dollar!" She kept yelling this until the young lad threw up his hands, and backed off with the best one-liner I have ever heard under the circumstances: "I no speak English," was his parting shot as he scurried away. Laughter and applause from Diane's party ensued, and she spent the rest of the cruise hearing her words played back by those new friends.

At our next morning breakfast, she asked me if I thought it would be okay to tell her husband the story when she got home. I told her I don't know how she could resist.

THAI TIE

In December 2004, we docked at Laem Chabang, the port that serves Bangkok, Thailand, and I was looking forward to escorting a tour into that fabulous city. But at the last moment, I was told my services would not be needed until the next day. That was okay with me. Later on when the tour I was supposed to escort returned, I could not believe the disillusionment among the guests. The one-and-a-half-hour trip to the city became two and a half hours, and the return trip was equally long. Lunch took over two hours, and that left only two hours to explore the wonders of Bangkok…not nearly enough by the standards of those who went. The traffic was horrendous due to construction, and there were massive amounts of commuting cars, trucks, bicycles, and motorbikes.

So, it was with dampened enthusiasm that I showed up the next morning for my escort reassignment. The word must have spread about the previous day's experience because we had only one bus with four guests, the driver, our guide Jamal, one bus boy, and me. We entered the city in one and a half hours with little traffic problems and no construction delays. Jamal ushered us into and through the Grand Palace, a magnificent collection of golden edifices protected by high walls. We spent about two and a half hours taking in the regal splendor of the spires, buildings, and the sights and sounds of the Thai culture. Then we went to the fabulous Shangri-La Hotel for a prompt and scrumptious lunch. From the beginning of the tour, Jamal kept eyeing my tote bag, which was typical of what many cruise lines provide to guests and staff. They come in handy for carrying cameras, mints, hand wipes, and a small first-aid kit that we escorts always carry in case of minor emergencies. As we were enjoying our lunch, Jamal asked how much one of those tote bags costs. As a gesture of good will, I unloaded the bag, stuffed my paraphernalia into a plastic bag, and presented the bag to him. Since there were very few tour guests, I thought it would be a little extra tip for him. He was overwhelmed and wanted to pay for the bag. I said, "No thanks." It was my pleasure for him to enjoy it. His smile was all the pay I needed.

We continued our day with a boat trip along the river where we could view many of the city's waterfront sights. Then we boarded our bus in the late afternoon and headed back to the ship. As I wished him luck and said good-bye, he handed me a little package and asked me to open it. "This is for you, Jim." It contained a beautiful maroon-and-yellow silk tie adorned with little elephants. We parted with handshakes and high fives. I can still see him waving with the tote bag over his shoulder as the bus pulled away. I was now the proud owner of a genuine "Thai tie."

Jumping ahead to December 2009, I was chatting on the phone with my friend Barbara about getting together for a little pre-Christmas dinner. My social schedule was much more flexible than hers, so I inquired as to her availability and a recommendation for a place to eat. We finally arrived at a date, time, and place. She suggested a Thai restaurant near her business. My mind instantly went back to my Bangkok experience, and I smiled. Over dinner, I told her the little story of my "Thai tie" experience. She said I should wear it the next time I visited this restaurant and tell the staff the story. I did.

COOL OR NOT?

I have met and worked with many dance hosts. They range in age from early fifties to early eighties. The majority is sixty and up. Teachers, engineers, pilots, lawyers, doctors, highway patrollers, bankers, accountants, real estate brokers, and military are just a few of the vocations represented. They are tall, medium, and short. They are slim and large. They are from everywhere, although there seems to be a preponderance of West Coast guys. They all have stories, agendas, and aspirations.

One of the caveats of being a host is not to fraternize exclusively with one lady. That is a rule that should not be broached. But it's naive to believe that this rule is followed all the time. Some hosts are extremely resourceful and can pull off a one-to-one relationship with a lady with absolute discretion. Others think they are cool and are about as obvious as one can be. But the one person neither type can fool for long is a fellow host, namely me. I take great pride and amusement in being able to sniff out their modus operandi.

Cabin mates Bill and Jack were two experts in the art of "relationship concealment," and what made it more unbelievable was they were both pulling it off on the same cruise. In fact, I am convinced to this day that I'm the only person who detected the game plan of these two wily veterans. Since it did not affect their performance and didn't put me in an uncomfortable position, I saw no reason to make a big deal about it. Indeed, it was the nearly flawless execution of their paying attention to all other ladies equally that aroused my suspicion that all was not quite as it appeared. The drama began on the second day of a fourteen-day cruise in the summer of 1996 to Alaska at the late-hour dance set.

I noticed that Bill was, from time-to-time, requesting that the band play certain songs. Nothing unusual there. But after each of these requests he would select the same lady, and they would do a very professional West Coast swing. This is a dance that you just don't do well with anybody who comes along. It takes some practice and a good "read" from each of the partners. I would not expect a lady chosen at random to be really good at it, particularly on the second day out. I tucked that piece of info into my brain and promised myself to see what happened the next night. Sure enough, the same thing happened. One time the lady actually was halfway out on the floor to dance before Bill even turned toward her. This was definitely not a first time encounter.

With Jack and his "never-knew-her-before" lady, it was the waltz. Every time a waltz played, they were on the floor. I decided to check this one out a little differently. I waited until Jack was off fetching a drink, and I asked the bandleader for a waltz. I asked "Jack's lady" to dance. She hesitated, said yes, but her heart wasn't in it. Now what was I to do with this newfound information? Should I have approached my two new buddies and told them that I was wise to their little game? I decided to play it straight and asked where they knew these ladies from. They both denied, with fervor, ever having met either of them before and wondered how I would ever get that impression. Now I was absolutely certain that something was going on and decided it was my duty (to myself) to get to the bottom of it.

As I was planning my next method of investigation, the mystery solved itself. Jack and Bill sought me out poolside the next afternoon. With wry smiles they admitted that, yes, they knew these ladies and had actually encouraged them to take this particular cruise so they could rendezvous. They wanted to know how I had come to that conclusion and who else knew. I said it was just a lucky guess, and I was sure no one else—passenger, staff, or crew—was aware of it. I just wanted them to know that as careful as they had been, they could not deceive "the rookie." I assured them that I wouldn't say anything to anybody and suggested they not even share the fact that I knew with the ladies in question. They told me if I wanted a little "privacy" from my cabin mate, I could use their cabin any time. They practically forced one of their cabin keys on me. With obvious smugness, they told me they weren't using it except to shower and change clothes anyway. Being a dance host can be a lot of fun.

BAND OF SISTERS

Deceptive, mean, selfish, ruthless, ill-mannered, stretcher of the truth. Over the years, I have witnessed these characteristics in particularly nasty individuals but never in an entire group of traveling companions. On a two-week cruise to Buenos Aires from Miami, a group of five ladies turned up with all these attributes. I touch elbows with many people from all over the world. The vast majority are very nice. But this group was as bad as it gets. Individually, these ladies may not have been so nasty, but a sort of "can-you-top-this" mentality developed as the cruise continued. Each new day seemed to sharpen the fangs of verbal abuse. Nobody was exempt. Waitresses, waiters, stewardesses, shore excursion people, front desk attendants, the cruise director, the maître d'hôtel, and of course, we hosts suffered under their wrath and displeasure. Here are some examples of what I witnessed and had to endure:

Marcie, the self-imagined timeless debutante, complained that the music was lousy, as we danced, and that the band couldn't keep a beat. This wasn't just on one dance but on every dance I had with her. That would be about two dances per night, or about thirty in all.

Ann, short and stocky, would always walk off the dance floor after about a third of the song. I have no idea why, but this behavior continued no matter whom she danced with.

Ruth, tall and painfully underweight, only did swing dances but still didn't want to miss a dance. So if it wasn't a swing number, she made it one, regardless of any attempt by her partner to lead her otherwise.

Bunny, a real misnomer if I ever heard one, would interrupt any conversation to claim a dance by pulling a host onto the floor even though he may have intended to favor another lady with a request. She came first.

Barbara, with the sweet southern drawl, would bless you with her thoughts of the shortcomings of others as she danced. Constant snipping and put-downs were her forte.

No matter how hard we tried, we four hosts could not draw a kind word or even a smile from any of these ladies. I dreaded our cruise-end ratings and, true to form, not one of us was exempt from the wrath of this "band of sisters."

FRANCISCO

As I travel the world, I encounter people other than cruise people. One such "land person" was Francisco. I first met him in Acapulco at a very upscale resort. After escorting tours from the ship to view the cliff divers and sop up the sights and sounds of Acapulco on two previous stops there, I decided I needed a change of scene. On the advice of a staff member aboard my ship, two of us took the seven-dollar cab ride to a posh hillside resort and prepared to enjoy an afternoon of sun, swimming, and margaritas. This very cheerful Mexican poolside waiter, Francisco, greeted us and provided us with lounges, towels, an umbrella, and all the attention that anyone could possibly ask for. His flashing eyes and broad smile were a warm welcome in this unfamiliar setting.

By the end of the afternoon, I knew Francisco was twenty-eight years old, married, had a small son, and lived nearby. As I left that day, I handed him my personal card, along with a tip for his afternoon of attentive service. He in turn thanked me and admired the tote bag I was carrying with the ship's name and logo. I offhandedly promised to return on my next stop in Acapulco.

As luck and fate would have it, I was back in Acapulco about a year later on the same ship. With a whole day to spend there, I looked for Francisco. On the outside chance that he was still at my favorite spa, I loaded down the tote bag he had admired with goodies such as razor blades, toothpaste, soap, shampoo, candy bars, chewing gum, and other incidentals that I thought Francisco and his family might need or enjoy. One of my fellow hosts, Charlie, accompanied me and off we were for a day of relaxation.

Sure enough there was Francisco. His smile broadened as he shouted "Jaime, over here!" He remembered my name. Later, I was able to convert the "Jaime" to "Hi-may," and it remains that to this day. The food was delicious, the drinks outstanding, and the attention we got from all the personnel at the resort was overwhelming. I believe Francisco had enlisted the aid of others on our behalf. Charlie asked me if I was part-owner of this place.

He said it was the best day he'd had in a long time. As we left, I handed Francisco the tote bag along with a generous tip and departed contented. The smile he returned was priceless and truly heartwarming.

I have been back to "Francisco's" four more times. Each time I took a "package" for Francisco and his family plus someone from the ship to share in the day. Normally it was one of my fellow hosts, but sometimes it was a passenger friend. Each one acknowledged, as Charlie did, that it was one of their best life experiences. Francisco was always at the center of activity concerning our enjoyment. He taught me the nuances of Mexican food, drink, and hospitality. I planned to see him as often as I could for the rest of my life. His friendly and unassuming approach to life and work served to remind me once again that it's people that make the difference. On my next stop to Acapulco, I again went to my favorite watering hole, but there was no Francisco. When I inquired about him, I was told he had moved on to another town and no one had seen him or heard from him. Too bad, but as far as I'm concerned my friend Francisco will always be there when I get the chance to stop by.

POOR LEWIS

There is no more considerate a gentleman than my friend Lewis. He is a great dancer and dresses immaculately. He is always in demand for host assignments. I have known him since he started going to sea about fifteen years ago. I always like it when he is aboard since he is the consummate host and is always on time and pulls his load. Over the years, he has made many friends among the dancing ladies and is sought for special parties that some of the guests throw. Some of these parties are very posh, and Lewis always presents a good appearance. He also volunteers for duties outside of his normal host role such as helping with group games. He is also brave and reverent, though occasionally moody. He normally gets high ratings and is visibly disturbed if he is not the top-rated host. In his own mind, I think, he considers himself slightly above his fellow teammates. This gets him in some hot water from time to time with his fellow hosts, but mostly with lady guests. Though we have a reporting chain to the cruise director through the dance instructor team, sometimes it doesn't work. For whatever reason, the cruise director may need to change something that affects us hosts. When this happens, it isn't always possible to go through the dance instructors to get us the message quickly. Since Lewis is well known, the cruise director may contact him and tell him to relay the message. Lewis then might get us together and say, "I just ran into the CD, and he wanted me to tell you guys…" The first time this happened there was no big reaction, but when it started becoming routine, some of the hosts start to think, "Is Lewis our new lead host? Why him and not me?" If they knew Lewis as well as I did, they would take no offense. But Lewis doesn't help himself with his delivery of the messages as though he's on the inside of the whole thing. So much for team building.

As for the ladies, on one recent cruise, Lewis got in the habit of escorting one woman who was a little bit feeble back to her stateroom at the end of the evening. Sometimes it was before the last set, and that was okay since he always returned in time for the next one. On the face of it, this is no big deal, even though it sends a bad message to other guests, (and his fellow hosts) of dispensing special treatment. Since he is a valued friend, I explained this to him. He said he understood but what was he to do? I told him he should ask a lady or another host to go with him, but Lewis kept up his personal escorting service. One evening he told me he was tired of it and would not be doing it anymore. I told him that would be like putting the toothpaste back in the tube. He dismissed my comment and at evening's end he told the lady he would not be walking her back and, without another word, abruptly left the area. Since this was a big departure from the special attention he had been paying to her, she asked us what she had done to offend Lewis. She was convinced that she had done something. She even began to tear up. We soothed her, and one of the remaining ladies accompanied her back to her stateroom. The next day, Lewis was in a dither. The lady had called to ask what had happened last night. He tried to explain, but it fell on deaf ears, so he went to the gift shop and got a card and a little stuffed dog. He wrote a note of apology and sent both, but it wasn't the same thereafter, and Lewis had dug himself a trench wide and deep.

Committing to a certain dance with a lady from New York was another seemingly innocent decision Lewis made several years ago. Over time, this became "their song" and lapsed over to future cruises they were both on. On one of these cruises the band played "their song," but Lewis had already invited a different lady to dance. His "normal" partner sat out the dance, even though she was asked by another host, and pouted. That did not go unnoticed by anyone who was paying attention.

As hosts we have to be ever alert for sensitivities of the ladies we dance and dine with. We also must be mindful of our duty to treat all ladies as equally as possible. A seemingly simple request by one of them can lead to long-term consequences we may not be prepared to endure.

THE BEST OF ALL THINGS

His name was Clint, and I knew at first sight he was a cut above the average well-off person aboard. His silver hair, bronzed body, and charming smile got my attention immediately. He was only outdone by his equally impressive wife, Irene, who still looked like the cheerleader she had obviously once been. Short blonde hair, slim waist, and a freckled face went well with her friendly demeanor. This forty-something couple from Vermont had boarded in Los Angeles about a month before and planned on staying on the ship for another two months.

Each morning I would see Clint on deck seated at a table deep in thought over his laptop with cell phone next to it. Some mornings I would see him talking to some far-off person as we sailed westward from Hawaii. He would always smile and wave. By noontime, he and Irene would be poolside sucking up the sun and sipping on cool drinks. Though I rarely saw them at dinner, I would see them at the entertainment in the show lounge each evening.

They were always seated at the same choice table adjacent to the stage.

One morning Clint did not seem to be too engrossed, so I asked if I could join him for a few minutes. He said, "Sure" as he closed the lid on the laptop. We chatted idly for a minute or so, and then I told him that he and Irene seemed to be enjoying their cruise, but I was intrigued by his morning ritual. He let out a loud laugh and told me a fascinating story that I had not heard before or since. He and Irene owned a small company in Vermont. He was actually "running" the company from the ship via cell phone and laptop computer.

Each year, they would take around three months off to see the world. But he would actually do all his work from aboard ship or in port via cell phone and laptop. He directed his home office personnel in major decisions that required his attention. His employees handled the daily details. It relieved him of the part of the business he didn't enjoy. In fact, he and Irene were going to try being away for three months twice next year. This couple had found a way to keep themselves and their employees very happy and the business, he told me, was more successful now than he'd ever imagined.

STILL HAD THE TOUCH

The place was Casablanca, Morocco, and I was escorting a land tour around the city. Our guide had just briefed us on the citadel in the Kasbah and given the group some free time to walk, shop, and eat as they desired. After a little stroll on my own buying a few souvenirs and engaging a few stall vendors in conversation, I headed for the meeting point where our bus would be awaiting us. As I rounded a corner, I came upon a group of six schoolboys shooting basketball. I judged them to be eight or nine years old. They were not that adept with this sport, but they were having a high-old time dribbling, shooting, and whooping it up. I really enjoy watching kids of all ages, and to see youngsters in Morocco playing basketball fascinated me. I stopped nearby and watched for a few minutes.

They all were decked out in oversized shirts sporting their favorite NBA star's name and number. Most of their shots never found the mark, but I applauded as one rattled off the rim and fell through. They all glanced at me and waved. I waved back, and the boy with the ball threw it to me. I stepped forward, caught it easily on the first bounce, took the old jump shot pose, and let one fly. All net. With that they applauded, and I bowed. The boy who retrieved my "swisher" started to throw it back to me, but I turned and ambled off with a wave of good-bye. The old saying is, "Walk away with them wanting more." Especially when lady luck is sitting on your shoulder.

WOULDN'T & COULDN'T

A cruise agent called in the summer of 1995 with a real plum of an assignment. I would be one of four hosts on a small ship bound for the Baltic Sea with about four hundred fifty guests, all from the New York area. These folks were devotees of a talk show on local radio there. I agreed, and on the appointed day flew to Oslo, Norway. The cruise would feature ports in Sweden, Finland, Estonia, Russia, and finish in Copenhagen, Denmark. The highlight was three days in St. Petersburg, Russia.

It became instantly apparent that my cabin mate, Steve, and I were the only host dancers aboard actually dancing. One host from Chicago didn't know he had to dance. He was told, he said, that he only needed to sit and chat with the ladies, play cards, and buy them drinks, and that's all he did. His cabin mate, Stanley, from Minnesota, acknowledged that he couldn't dance very well, so rather than embarrass himself he decided not to dance either. I just shook my head and waited for the axe to fall on them. Steve, a great guy from Philadelphia, and I carried the "dance load" as best we could and kept smiling. Surely, we felt, the cruise director, Gretchen, would straighten this thing out. She was a German lady in her mid forties who seemed quite adept at her job but was a bit overwhelmed by the New Yorkers and their demands.

About the third day out, she called me to her office to tell me that two of the hosts weren't even dancing. That I already knew. She told me I needed to do something about it. Since all of us were paying our agent for the privilege of taking this cruise, I didn't feel it was my job to straighten things out, and I told her so. I assured her that Steve and I would cover all the dance sets, whether assigned or not, and continue to do what we were there for. She thanked me. Things continued with Steve and me dancing. Strangely, we heard no complaints from the passengers or the cruise director. When we reached St. Petersburg, all of the passengers were flying to Moscow for the day. The ship's tour manager called to advise Steve and me that we two were invited to go as a reward for our extra efforts. Several nights later, we were asked by the leader of the New York group to attend a gala for the entire party. Guess who wasn't present?

THE COST OF A KISS

K al, Clarence, and I landed one morning at Santiago International airport in Pudahel, Chile, which is about ten miles from downtown. We hailed a cabbie and gave him the address of our hotel where we were to spend the night before boarding a ship in Valparaiso the next morning. The taxi driver spoke passable English with a Spanish accent and was very friendly. I asked him the best way to find a guide to give us a tour of the city since we had the whole afternoon and evening free. Our driver, Eduardo, a married man with three grown children, said he would be willing to do that, and we negotiated a price for five hours.

After checking in to our hotel, and having lunch, we met Eduardo. Santiago is a beautiful city of about five million people, and its architecture has a Spanish influence. Our first stop was the Church of St. Francis. A church stop seems to be on every tour no matter where in the world you go. The church was huge and very opulent. Eduardo whispered that "kisses" here were not readily available. Our next stop was out of town at the Club Hipico de Santiago Racetrack, a venue with grandstands worthy of patrons dressed in formal attire. Thoroughbred horse racing is very popular in Chile. The all-grass track was impeccably manicured, and the horses that were being worked out used a separate course. They snorted and pranced as if demanding our attention. Eduardo said that a "kiss" here was very expensive and only available during racing hours. By this time we were beginning to understand what our guide meant by a kiss. He was referring, of course, to the price of a lady escort. Our entertainment on the way back became asking Eduardo for the price of a kiss at this point and that.

A stop for coffee was in order, so Eduardo suggested café con piernas (coffee with legs.) The café we entered was small and offered coffees of all kinds served by attractive young ladies in skimpy attire. The coffee cost two dollars, but for thirty dollars, you could get a kiss as well, Eduardo offered. He said there were hundreds of similar cafés in the city and the coffee was excellent. Not all offered the kiss option. We stopped for a music concert in the Plaza de Armes and soaked up the culture. No mention of a kiss here, though. There was one last place Eduardo wanted us to see—the US embassy. Though we couldn't enter and no pictures were allowed, we did make a short stop. As we happily sped off, Eduardo anticipated our question and said the cost of a kiss in this neighborhood was two hundred dollars any time of day or night.

We speculated afterward what must have led Eduardo to conclude that we "gringos" needed kiss information. Maybe he thought we looked "undernourished."

COLLEAGUES

I would be remiss if I didn't say a little about the great guys I share dance host duties with. There may have been as many as fifty different fellows I sailed with over the years—some just once, others a few times, and still others many times. As one might expect, these gentlemen were from all across the United States, Canada, and even some from England. Each one brings different social skills to the position and different dance talents. The thing they have in common though is their desire to travel. Let me tell you about three of them. One has passed on, one shifted from being a host to a destination lecturer, and the third is still active but his legs have worn out, so he doesn't ballroom dance much anymore.

I met Jim on a transatlantic cruise from Tilbury, England, to New York. He had retired from a teaching position at a college in the San Francisco area. His expertise was in psychology. He had also retired from a marriage consulting business there. His goal was to touch foot in all the countries of the world, and when I met him he was well on his way to doing just that. Our friendship was cemented early when he advised me, authoritatively, that you couldn't have two Jims on a cruise, so I would be James. I told him that his being five-foot-eight compared to my six feet didn't buy him that decision-making latitude, but since he was obviously older and had more hosting experience, I would cut him a break and be James. I added that everybody gets one free shot at me, and he had just used up his. We laughed, and things went well thereafter. After that cruise he sent me cards from all over the world addressed to Jim/James, until his passing some twelve years later.

About midway in our friendship, we were assigned to another cruise out of San Francisco. He called and invited me to come three days early and stay with him. I did and he showed me San Francisco from one end to the other—the Japanese Tea Garden, Beach Blanket Babylon Playhouse, Fisherman's Wharf, the Bay Bridge, and onward to the Napa Valley for winery tours. These were just a smidgen of the places we went. I told him we spent a week together in three days. His sons advised me of his death, and by that time I think Jim had managed to visit almost every country in the world. I learned to appreciate travel and its limitless opportunities from him. I told his sons the Jim/James story, and they enjoyed that.

Niki and I met early in my hosting career and he was brand new. He told me that the cruise line had advised him to attach himself to me and I'd teach him the ropes of being a dance host. I told him, as I would tell any host, to just be himself, and if he had any specific question I'd be happy to explain what I'd do in that situation. The secret to doing a good job is a function of following a few basic cruise line rules, using good manners, and trusting the upbringing you had as a child. If your gut tells you something is not going well, then it's probably not, and you should seek advice. Niki was a popular host and kept detailed journals of his travels. He also took loads of pictures at the ports where we stopped. I've been to England, Fiji, Australia, and Norway with Niki, and we would tread the streets together. I always had fun when aboard with Niki. As I do with many of my host friends, he and I exchange Christmas cards. Sometime around 2005, I flew to Costa Rica to board a ship and, lo and behold, there was Niki. He was no longer a dance host, but a destination lecturer. He had parlayed his journal and photos of his travels around the world into presentations. I attended his lecture on Machu Picchu. It was polished, informative, and accurate. His personality was as I remembered. No one who met him could forget his charming manner and easy conversation style. So Niki hung up his dancing shoes and is now making presentations of destinations the cruise ships are headed. When I last got an email from him in 2010, he was spending about ten months a year traveling and lecturing. Niki taught me to take a relaxed and easygoing approach to having fun in all types of places and situations.

In 1990, John was one of the original sea-going dance hosts with a cruise line out of San Francisco. When I first met him in the fall of 1992, the word "Mr. G.Q." popped into my mind. As it turns out, not only did he dress immaculately, but he had spent his career as a salesman of men's clothing for a high-end clothier. We were teamed up and hit it off immediately. Since I was new at this game, I would watch what he was doing or not doing and take my lead from him. I never told him this until years later. John was well liked and very sought after for assignments since he was exactly the type of person the cruise lines were looking for to represent them. He was a good dancer, a wonderful conversationalist, and an all-around good guy. Plus, you could cut bread with the creases in his pants. His ascots always matched his pocket handkerchief. His shoes were polished to a patent leather-type luster, and his clothes fit perfectly. Some would have said too perfectly. He knew all the nuances of host behaviors, and it turned out there were more than I could have ever imagined. *Don't walk around the ship carrying a glass of anything. If you're in one of the lounges, sit at a table, not at the bar. When walking or dancing, keep the jacket buttoned.* According to John, there were no "laws" stating these things, but the first impressions we hosts make is very important to our success. John taught me that the service we provide should not be taken for granted. He is really retired now, in Arizona, and keeps fit walking and teaching line dancing. I'm told he is the consummate host on land, and that is not at all hard to believe.

PAYBACK

Modern-day cruising finds an unusual number of single, divorced, and widowed women traveling alone compared to like "situationed" men. It is a safe, convenient, and adventurous way for women to enjoy a vacation and see the world. As a dance host, I am fortunate to meet all kinds of women from everywhere and hear lots of stories. The ladies like to talk on the dance floor, at lunch, or over a pre-dinner cocktail. One particular lady, Joanne, comes to mind, for it makes a point that I fear is too often the case.

Joanne was from the southwest—Phoenix, I think. Highly educated, articulate, and ramrod straight, her five-foot-nine-inch frame exuded confidence, and she could seem intimidating. She was a fair but enthusiastic dancer. She enjoyed many of the shore excursions offered by the cruise line. She was an outgoing conversationalist and always seemed to have an experience or a point of view to share. I got to know Joanne pretty well on a three-cruise assignment in the South Pacific area. One afternoon I spotted her on deck and stopped to say hello. She asked me to sit and chat a while. I listened to her talk about her travels. She had been all over the world, it seemed. She had been traveling extensively for the five years since her husband had passed away. She told me she spends about eleven months of the year at sea, and she could afford the best accommodations and services. She loved the shows and variety acts on the ship. She used the computers aboard to track her finances. She danced and ate the finest foods. She used the gym, the beauty salon, and played bridge.

There was hardly a minute in the day that she didn't fill. As she paused for a breath, I asked her if she had family at home. She got a wistful look in her eyes as she told me she had one daughter who lived near her home in Phoenix. As if anticipating my next question, she blurted out that for a time after her husband died she didn't travel. She would call her daughter from time to time, but she was always too busy to include Joanne in her life. I thought I detected sadness in her voice when she added, "She never calls." But in an instant her mood changed to a mischievous grin and she said, "My daughter's inheritance is the price she pays. I hope she can afford it."

ONE MAN'S TRASH IS
ANOTHER MAN'S TRASH

In late summer 2001, I was escorting a group of twenty-eight cruise ship guests while in Venice, Italy. We took a boat to the island of Murano to tour the famous glass factory there. We alit from our small craft, and our guide led the group toward the glass factory buildings. As part of my responsibilities as escort, I was to ensure that I had the group assembled for a glass blowing demonstration. I was missing some people, so I backtracked to where we had left the boat. Near our landing dock was a debris area about eight feet by twenty feet surrounded by a small fence where unsalable glass products were accumulated for later disposal or re-melting by the glass factory. There I found three of my "sheep" (all ladies) pilfering through the throwaways to gather discarded pieces of glass. Some pieces came easy, but others needed to be dug for. They were oblivious to the fact that the group had moved on. They were not about to interrupt their expedition for discarded "gold" to witness the artisan who gave a most interesting demonstration of the art of glass blowing. Since I now knew where they were, I left them to their treasure hunt.

Eventually they caught up to the group, but only after the demo was over and the shopping opportunities were going on. So, back to the pile of rubbish they went to continue their quest for treasure on property they were visiting as invited guests. My embarrassment by the behavior of my fellow travelers was only overshadowed by my wondering how they might feel if a person foreign to them should pull up to their home and sift through their garbage that they had placed at the curb in front of their home. I guess I'll never really know, but I guess they would not be as charitable with invasion of their space and discarded property as their Venetian hosts had been.

POOR BOYS

I have observed an interesting behavior among some of the passengers on ships where I have been a dance host. They know or can figure out that we are essentially on for a "free ride." Many then jump to the conclusion that since that is the case we all must be destitute, on food stamps, or otherwise down on our luck.

The truth is that most of the gentlemen I have sailed with are retired from worthwhile jobs or businesses. They were gainfully employed as doctors, lawyers, accountants, engineers, and teachers. They were shop owners, clothiers, architects, military retirees, and of course dance instructors. Most of them are, at the very least, modestly successful, and a few are actually very wealthy. In all cases they are well-educated either through formal education or life's experiences. Most cruise lines publish biographies of their hosts in the onboard newspaper. I have been approached many times by passengers who want to talk about my background, and it seems to me that these folks have been impressed by what they have read.

An interesting situation arose for my host friend Jason several years ago. A very exotic lady from Reno, Nevada, took a shine to him. As he tried to deflect her obvious attachment to him he explained that though he was flattered, our non-favoritism commitment made it impossible for him to pay special attention to any one lady. Without missing a beat, the lady announced to him that when he got off the ship she would send him a first-class airline ticket so he could afford to visit her. Jason, unbeknownst to her or others, had been a very successful real estate developer in Florida before he retired and became a poor dance host.

So Noted

I wonder what, if any, impact we dance hosts have upon the folks we meet on the ships. I place a high priority on doing everything I can to help the guests have the cruise of their life. In our position as hosts, that might be just as simple as showing a lady where the beauty salon is located. It might be extra attention paid to an elderly gentleman who is having a little trouble stepping down from the bus on a land tour. I take great pride in being an extra set of eyes, ears, and hands when it comes to ensuring no opportunity to help some guest in need goes unattended. From time to time I have gotten little notes of appreciation from people I have met and have paid some little courtesy to. The following in her own words is an example of this.

From Penni: Dearest Jim, thank you so much for making my birthday so special. It was very kind of you to host the wine and champagne for lunch, but most of all thank you for joining me for lunch. It is always a pleasure to be in your company.

I have known Penni for several years, and she always seems to be alone. Though she dances, she wasn't a regular at our dance sets. Those times when we did talk, she would reminisce about her younger years. Since I knew her birthday, I decided to surprise Penni with a little birthday luncheon with a few of us hosts. She was surprised, and the note she sent me was my reward.

This was one of over thirty such notes I have received over the years, and they all remind me of why it is we gentleman are placed on cruise ships. Though dancing is our main reason for being aboard, I believe being helpful and just plain friendly comes with the territory. Most of my colleagues agree, and I'm sure they could produce notes of thanks or appreciation they have gotten in their travels. Even if I don't receive written acknowledgement, I know from the smile, the nod, or the thumbs up that my help was appreciated, and I feel relevant.

SPEAKING ENGLISH EVERYWHERE

On a land tour in South America, I disembarked our crude river boat in the small town of Garu on the upper reaches of the Amazon River, about fifty miles south of Iquitos, Ecuador. This village was typical of many I'd visited except that in this one I was in for a surprise. As "Norte Americanos" our arrival was anxiously awaited by the local students. Their assignment was to interview each of the twenty members of our group, in English. Two students, a boy and a girl, around the age of twelve or thirteen, approached me. They had a list of questions written in Spanish. They asked each one in English as best they could. Sometimes I understood, other times I didn't. I have a small knowledge of Spanish, so I interjected some when I could. They thought this was really funny and, before long, there was a small group of adult onlookers cheering on their efforts and tee-heeing at my feeble attempts to converse in Spanish. Their questions were typical of what you might expect: Where do you live? How old are you? Do you have any children? It went on for perhaps fifteen minutes and ended with, "Do you have e-mail?" (A caution flag went up for me at this point.)

Evidentially, they wanted to keep in touch. Some of the group went for this. I politely declined based on advice of others who had wished they had declined such an invitation.

They had a doughnut-type pastry they offered us, and I tried some. I sat and asked them questions, in English, about themselves. Our guide pried me away from these wonderful children so she could get on with the rest of our tour. I left with a sense of win-win with these children. I certainly felt I learned as much about them as they had about me. I have had similar experiences with children in other parts of the world. China, Costa Rica, and Bhutan come to mind. In every case, it was rewarding and educational for me and, I hope, for the children. They were always respectful, humorous, and eager to expand their knowledge of the English language and our culture. The more I travel, the more I realize, kids are kids everywhere you go.

DRINK UP

All cruise lines, with large ships or small, are constantly trying to provide passengers with the things that bring them back. It is quite apparent that great food, plentiful beverages, top entertainment, and impeccable service, all in a friendly atmosphere, are the hallmarks of successful cruise lines. The plentiful beverages have always caught my interest. Over the years I have found that people's drinking habits are telling. Some of the upscale cruise lines now include alcoholic beverages as part of the total cruise cost. Therefore any reasonable type of alcoholic beverage available is "free." In my experience I have not witnessed but one instance where a passenger on one of these ships was "over-served."

On most cruise lines, complimentary drinks are served on the outdoor deck on a sail away from a port. The music plays, the banners wave, and the drinks of the day flow freely as the passengers wave at real or imaginary friends standing on the dock.

Some of the favorite servings at sail away are mai tais, margaritas, bloody Marys, mimosas, and fruit punch. Pisco sours are a favorite in Chile and Peru. Champagne is served many times on a sail away from ports where new passengers have just boarded. Another favorite time for serving complimentary drinks is when the liner is slowly traversing special places that attract many passengers to sightseeing on deck. The Panama Canal, the Suez Canal, and sailing into Stockholm, Sweden are examples of this.

Whereas the typical drinks as mentioned are appropriate in most places, this is not so for the chillier climates of say, Antarctica. Hot chocolate seems to be a favorite there. On a cruise in those waters out of Punta Arenas, Chile, the cruise line treated everyone on deck to hot chocolate laced generously with dark rum. I had never tasted this spiced up concoction before, but I can assure you at sea or on land, cocoa and rum is a real winner on a chilly winter day. The combination of a couple of these treats with chilly weather and then walking into a warm interior of a ship can bring a blush to the cheek of most anyone.

REX

The dictionary defines peripatetic as, "carried on while moving or walking from one place to another." Well Rex should have his picture next to that definition. His philosophy is if it's worth doing, then it's worth doing at full speed. As a host he literally runs to ask ladies to dance. He runs to be the greeter at the door. He runs to hold a chair for a person. It is all well intentioned, and I truly believe he doesn't have a bad bone in his body. He is multi-talented as well. Besides being a good dancer, he plays the piano, and does so to amuse guests as they wait to have their tours called. He speaks eloquently, albeit a tad wordy, and is always there to help with anything that needs to be done. His casual daily attire is normally complete with an alpine type hat complete with feather. His formal attire includes attention-getting ruffled tux shirts accompanied by a loudly colored bow tie and cummerbund.

Rex spends an inordinate amount of energy meeting people and recording their names so he can greet them by name the next time he sees them. This, of course, is admirable but it appears to be a forced effort rather than just courtesy. Even when he is not scheduled for a dancing event, he shows up with great fanfare, which does not endear him to his fellow hosts. The bottom line is that it usually appears that Rex is maneuvering to attract all the attention so that everyone will think that he is the host with the most. His whirling dervish behavior is designed to assure that he continues to get assignments from the cruise line. He admitted as much to me when I tried to explain the effect his over-actions can have.

What Rex had not yet figured out is that when you upstage other hosts it causes resentment within the ranks, and that detracts from the team's overall effort to assure that the passengers have a wonderful cruise. Terms like "showboating," "one-upmanship," "apple polisher," and "show off" start creeping into conversations, unbeknownst to him. Also, the cruise staff, which has a great deal to say about whether a dance host is asked back for subsequent cruises, may not give him high marks. That is mostly because Rex does not fit the mold of a good team player. Individualism is fine but within the framework of decorum that has the appearance of being under control. "Low-key is best key," is my motto.

I have always gotten along with Rex, and he has always treated me fine. In recent correspondence with me, he expressed disappointment that he was selected for just one cruise for the upcoming year. He said he had requested seven. Frankly, I was surprised he got any. He sent me a nine-page collection of write-ups from newspapers about his accomplishments and accolades ashore. He asked me, quite pointedly, what he was doing wrong host wise. Since I wouldn't have relied on him should we be assigned together on a future cruise, I felt no overpowering need to share my total feelings, so I replied, "Maybe you should concentrate on what other hosts are doing right."

MIXED MESSAGES

Many cruise lines rely on feedback from passengers to evaluate their successes. Though these ratings can be helpful to identify areas of needed improvement, sometimes they are used to gauge the effectiveness of key shipboard personnel. Rightly or wrongly, a fair or poor rating in one area, say food service, is viewed as a reflection on the maître d' hotel. Likewise, a rating of excellent would be attributed to his outstanding skills.

On an Alaskan cruise in 1994, we six newly boarded dance hosts were in attendance at the cruise director, Lawrence's, typical meeting with his entertainment department. He was upset and it showed. It so happened that on the previous cruise the passengers were not happy with the entertainment package he offered and so stated on their cruise-end comment sheets. Using this as a basis, he berated the entire group for the results, and it was obvious that he took this as a personal failure on his part.

In particular, many of the unescorted ladies who were dancers complained about the dance hosts, so he quickly zeroed in on us six even though none of us had been aboard for that last cruise. His words were stern, and his meaning was clear when he said, "I don't care what you guys do or how you do it, but I don't want to hear or read one complaint from the ladies you dance with on this cruise." The stifled, but audible, chuckles from the rest of the entertainment staff punctuated his comment. This instruction, of course, was in direct contradiction to our normal instruction to pay no "special attention" to the ladies we dance with.

No complaints, to my knowledge, were registered by any of the ladies we danced with. I know that I did not favor any one lady with special attention and though I have no firsthand knowledge that any of my colleagues did, I suspect they did not either. At the next cruise director's meeting, at the beginning of the next cruise, he complimented us hosts for doing our job in an outstanding manner since he received no complaints from the ladies who danced with us. Of course the chuckles from the rest of the entertainment department were not stifled this time, and the cruise director just smiled and threw us a wink.

No Fly Zone

John and Renee are longtime cruisers and love to dance. They are a very reserved Chinese couple from Hong Kong. I have sailed with them many times and have grown to know them very well. We have become very good friends. I acknowledge them each time I see them and have a pleasant conversation with them as time allows. They always occupy a table near the bandstand and confine their dancing to an area within about six feet of the band. We more seasoned hosts have come to expect to see them in that area and are sure to give them plenty of room. Their dancing style is unique and is one I am not familiar with, but they seem to know what they are doing and enjoy themselves even though they like to have their own little space. We have come to know the area where they dance as a "no fly zone." Being a repeat cruiser, John has the ear of the cruise director, and he does not hesitate to express his opinions, both good and bad, about the music, the band, and of course the dance hosts. His input is taken seriously since returning guests are the lifeblood of most cruise lines.

One of the cardinal rules of dancing is to display proper dance etiquette at all times. While this is good advice for all dancing couples, it applies particularly to dance hosts as we maneuver our partners around the floor. To ignore the common courtesies of dance can sometimes lead to dire consequences.

In early 2006 on a cruise in the Far East, such an instance occurred when a rather new host routinely invaded John and Renee's dancing space, as well as that of other couples. In his attempt to make himself look good, he was weaving his partner in and out of couples on the floor and not being very careful, let alone polite, in his dancing. Several of us hosts saw this, and at the first opportunity we approached Josh and nicely filled him in on the history of John and Renee and how it was best to avoid the small area they always danced in. Josh took exception to our suggestion and said, "Hey, I like to use the whole floor, and I can't be looking out for other couples all the time."

Soon the inevitable happened and Josh bumped into John and Renee and had close calls with a few other couples. Once again we nicely cautioned him and once again he shrugged off our efforts to save him from embarrassment or worse. On the last night of the cruise, I said good-bye to John and Renee and wished them a safe trip home. John took me aside and told me that one of my colleagues didn't deserve to be a dance host and he most likely would not be one for long if he had anything to say about it. About two weeks after I completed my tour aboard the ship, I received an e-mail from a fellow host telling me he heard that the cruise line told Josh his services as a dance host were no longer required. I couldn't help but wonder if Josh crashed and burned in part because he continually entered the no fly zone. A rather hard landing for one who could have easily executed a fly by and landed safely at another location.

THE AUTHOR

GLACIER BAY, ALASKA - 1994

ATLAS SAID HE WOULD HELP

NORTH CAPE, NORWAY - 2000

ALFRED THE GREAT

MOMBASSA, KENYA - 1996

I'LL HAVE MINE ON THE ROCKS

GIBRALTER, U.K. - 2009

THIS MIME LEFT ME SPEECHLESS

LAS RAMBLAS, BARCELONA, SPAIN - 2001

BUT YOU SAID IT WOULDN'T HURT

ELEPHANT CAMP, PHUKET, THAILAND - 2001

5ᵀᴴ PLACE, YOU'VE GOT TO BE KIDDING

CRYSTAL HARMONY DANCE CONTEST - 1996

LET'S SEAL THIS DEAL

GALAPOGAS ISLANDS, EQUADOR - 2005

HAVE PACKAGES? I'LL *"TOTE-EM"*

VANCOUVER B.C., CANADA - 2004

WE WILL BE OPEN IN A MINUTE

CRYSTAL SERENITY - 2012

DARCO AND I MAKE THE LINGUINI

CIVIAVECCHIA, ITALY FARMHOUSE B & B - 2010

HORSING AROUND

PINTADA, HONDURAS - 2010

FRANCISCO, MI AMIGO

VILLA VERA, ACAPULCO, MEXICO - 1996

"KISSING ANNIE" WITH CAPTURED PREY

S. S. ROTTERDAM V - 1997

THIS PLACE IS REALLY COOL!

ICE BAR, STOCKHOLM, SWEDEN - 2008

IN LINE FOR JUST A BOWL OF RICE

GREAT WALL, BEIJING, CHINA - 2000

VISITING HERE WAS NOT POINTLESS

THE PYRAMID OF CHEOPS
GIZA, EGYPT - 2001

SPLISH SPLASH WHAT A BATH

OHCO RIO FALLS, JAMACIA - 1999

ONE WAY TO GET CROWNED

HO CHI MINH CITY, SOUTH VIET NAM - 2011

THE HOST DREAM TEAM

CRYSTAL SERENITY - 2003 (L TO R) ED, RICHARD, ME & BOB

DR. DRAGON, I PRESUME

KOMODO ISLAND, INDONESIA - 2011

LET'S HAVE A BARREL OF FUN

MYCENEA WINERY, NAVPLION, GREECE - 2012

NOW THERE'S A REAL DANISH PASTRY

COPENHAGEN, DENMARK - 1994

SING ALONG WITH US

STREET SINGER, AUCKLAND, NEW ZEALAND - 2007

YOUR MECHANIC LIVES WHERE?

FRANZ JOSEPH GLACIER, NEW ZEALAND - 2007

SADLY, IT ISN'T BLUE

BLUE MOSQUE, ODESSA, UKRAINE - 2012

FROM THE TOP LOOKING "DOWN-UNDER"

HARBOUR BRIDGE, SYDNEY, AUSTRALIA - 2005

SAMSON I AM NOT

QUEEN VICTORIA GARDENS
MELBOURNE, AUSTRALIA - 2003

STAIRWAYS TO THE TSARS

POTEMKIN STAIRS, ODESSA, UKRAINE - 2012
192 STEPS

DO THE FLOWERS MEAN WE'RE ENGAGED?

BLOODY MARY'S, BORA BORA - 2008

I'M AN HOUR EARLY? GUESS THE YOKE'S ON ME

PARADE FLOAT, MIJAS SPAIN - 2011

HOW'S THE WEATHER DOWN THERE MON?

GRAND TURK ISLAND - 2010

KISS WHAT? WHERE?

COUNTY CORK, IRELAND, BLARNY STONE - 2003

I'M NOT STEPPING OUT TODAY!

MACHU PICCHU, PERU - 2004

THESE FILLIES ARE WINNERS

MANORAS RACE TRACK
MONTEVIDEO, URUGUAY - 2007

WHICH WAY TO GO, NORTH OR SOUTH?

ON THE EQUATOR IN EQUADOR - 2005

WHERE TO NOW KIDDO?

CAPE OF GOOD HOPE, SOUTH AFRICA - 2006

DON'T TOW THESE VINTAGE MODELS

MONTE CARLO, MONACO - 2012

ZIPPIDY DO DAH

COSTA RICAN ZIP LINE - 1998

OSIRIS SAID,
"STAY FOR DINNER, WE'RE HAVING FISH"

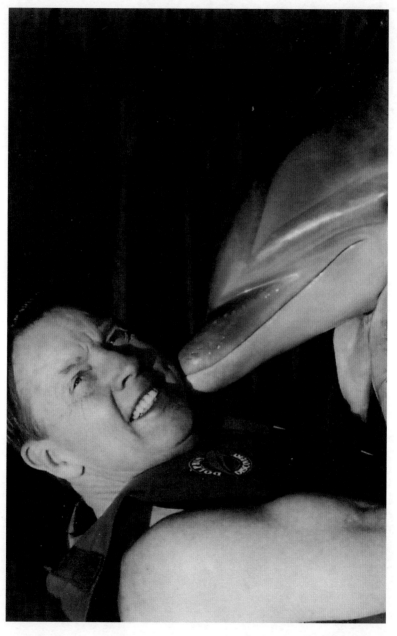

TOTOLA, BRITISH VIRGIN ISLANDS - 2000

THE THREE "SUDSA-TEERS"

ME, DAVID, & NIKI
SAVA SAVA, FIJI - 1997

WHAT A LUCKY GUY AM I

PAT AND ME, CRYSTAL SYMPHONY - 1997

Two Brothers

There they stood—two well-dressed, smiling guys in their mid forties at the fifth deck bar on an upscale cruise liner sailing out of Barcelona. Being a proper host suggests I search out single men early in a cruise so that I may introduce them to unattached ladies at the earliest opportunity. That being the case, I introduced myself to David and Gary. I briefly explained, while pointing to my name tag, who I was and my role for the rest of their twelve-day cruise. They were familiar with "host programs" and assured me they would be delighted to become acquainted with some eligible ladies. We chatted long enough for me to determine they were brothers and Canadian citizens. I excused myself with the promise to "bend an elbow" with them later.

The next day, there was a party for all persons who were traveling independently. I noticed David and Gary were not there. Later, they told me that they had opted to attend a presentation on the United Nations, which was running concurrently with the "singles thing." They figured that since I now knew who all the eligible ladies were I could guide them in the correct direction as occasion dictated. Nice move on their part. These brothers were clever as well as personable.

Later that day at afternoon tea, I sat with Gary and chatted some more. It turned out his ex-wife was a horsewoman. Now I know next to nothing about horses, so I asked some questions. He completely overwhelmed me with terms such as tack, dressage, and stadium jumping. Surprisingly, I became interested to the point where I read up on the sport so I could at least enjoy a conversation about it. I learned that this is not a sport for the financially faint of heart.

My next encounter with the brothers was on one of the land tours that the cruise ship sponsored. I exchanged some pleasantries with them, and they indicated that they did not realize that escorting tours was one of my responsibilities. I explained that ship sponsored excursions normally included a person who acted as a liaison with the tour operator. Many times a host does that job. I noticed with interest that the "boys" were accompanying two of the single lady passengers from Puerto Rico. These guys didn't need any help.

Over the next several days, as our schedules allowed, David, Gary, and I spent quality time together over wine, coffee, and piña coladas. The ladies from Puerto Rico always seemed to be around them as well.

I was surprised when the cruise director asked me to be available one afternoon for an interview. He explained there was a travel writer onboard who was doing an article on the ship, its offerings, and some of its personnel. Imagine my shock to be met by David at the appointed hour. He interviewed me for about two hours. It included pictures and a promise to send me a copy of the article when it was released. I asked him how it felt to keep his mission a secret when I was trying so hard to see that he had a great cruise experience. He said it was fun, and he and Gary had great chuckles when he decided after our first meeting that I would be one of the people interviewed. He indicated he wanted to see how the whole operation really was when people didn't know what he was up to. I had to agree, as I noted that one really never knows in a new situation with new people what is going on. It is another good reason to be yourself all the time. Even though David had one-upped me, I sent him the wonderful picture I took of him and his brother with the Puerto Rican senoritas. I wondered if he would include that in his article. True to his word, he sent me a copy. I was flattered with the portion that applied to me. It still makes for a pleasant memory when I refer to it. As it turned out, this was not my last encounter with media aboard cruise liners.

EXCEPTION

On a trip to Copenhagen, Denmark, I was asked to report to the cruise director at my "earliest convenience." When someone uses that terminology I've learned that means "right now."

He asked me to have a seat and then told me he had a special assignment for me that would take about four hours the next day while we were in port. He explained that one of the unescorted ladies had requested an escort to see the sights, have lunch, and do a little shopping. He indicated that he wanted me to do that. I told him I would rather not be put in this potentially embarrassing position since the other ladies and host would eventually find out. He smiled and said he understood perfectly but that I shouldn't worry since I would be doing this with his blessing and he would handle any fallout. He was a good guy, and I took him at his word. The conversation ended when I asked how I was chosen to be the lucky guy. He said, "Because she asked specifically for you." It seems that Inez, who I had danced many times with, felt very comfortable around me and also sensed we had some interests in common.

I met Inez in the lobby after breakfast the next morning, and we set out to see Copenhagen. A stunning grey-haired lady about five feet-eight inches tall. A grin as wide as ever I saw was topped by a set of mischievous blue eyes. She told me she would like to walk into town instead of taking the shuttle bus. That was okay with me. We strolled down the pier and through the stone exit gate and found the pathway into the city. I had been in Copenhagen before, and armed with the tourist map I was sure we wouldn't get lost.

We soon found ourselves abreast of the famous "Little Mermaid" atop her rock in the harbor, and we took pictures. We then found ourselves at the Gefion's Fountain with its team of four oxen who were the sons of Gefion. This is Copenhagen's largest monument.

While we walked Inez told me of her home and her love of travel and seeing new sights. We turned inland and visited the National Gallery and then the Botanical Gardens. For lunch we had a local specialty, an-open faced sandwich called a smorrebrod, in a sidewalk restaurant. It consisted of fresh lettuce on buttered bread topped with shrimp, liver pate, and bacon. Of course, a glass of beer from the nearby Carlsberg brewery was mandatory. After lunch, we took a bus back to the port where we continued our outing at the Waterfront Shopping Mall. Around 2:30 p.m., laden with full stomachs and some packages, we boarded the ship. I promptly reported to the cruise director "mission accomplished" and handed him the bill for lunch. He smiled and thanked me for making his job a little easier.

Since the ship was overnighting in Copenhagen, an evening at the famous Tivoli Gardens was offered to the passengers. We hosts were to act as bus escorts. This was great because we got free time after our arrival at Tivoli until our bus was to return. As I stepped off the bus at the gate to Tivoli Gardens, there was Inez and three of her lady friends from the ship. They latched on to me and asked if I could and would be their guide for the evening. What could I do? We listened to a great jazz concert, we shopped, and walked the Gardens. Around 11:00 p.m. they agreed they needed something to eat, so we found a little outdoor café and had pastries and espresso. I had a beer—Carlsberg, of course. Around 12:30 a.m. I finally got my four charges aboard the bus and back to the ship.

Next morning I ran into the cruise director and told him of my adventure. He laughed and said, "Hey, that's why you get the big bucks." His smile didn't even fade when I gave him the bill for the pastries, espressos, and beer. Exceptions make the rule, I guess. I get a Christmas card from Inez every year, with a picture of her from one of her travels.

GOLDEN THREADS OF FRIENDSHIP

It was about twelve years ago that I met Maureen on a cruise ship sailing the Suez Canal. She was a petite blond with a great smile and a shy demeanor. I was a dance host, and she was a recent widow. Though I remembered her vaguely when I sailed with her again four years later, I had no idea what was about to evolve. As we danced on the first evening, Maureen told me she had something to tell me when we had a few minutes alone. So over a morning breakfast, she told me that she had never forgotten our first meeting and hoped one day we would meet again so she could tell me about the impact I'd had on her life as a result. She said that she had been feeling really low and sorry for herself when we first met. Being a recent widow, she was very reluctant to expose herself to new situations and was only onboard at the insistence of her family. She related to me how I had befriended her and encouraged her to participate in the nightly dancing. I had also seen to it that she was introduced to the other hosts and the ladies who were also at the dancing venues.

Apparently this was the little extra kindness that allowed her to come out of her self-imposed shell. I was amazed that after four years she would have remembered the situation and could explain it to me so vividly. Of course I was flattered by her story and felt good about the fact I had impacted her life in such a manner, albeit unknown to me for those years. Throughout the rest of the cruise, Maureen told several passenger of our original encounter, so I continued to hear about it during our time at sea. I made sure I got Maureen's address, phone number, and e-mail. I didn't want to wait another four years to talk to her. We exchanged Christmas cards yearly thereafter and actually sailed together a few more times. Each time we saw each other, our unspoken greeting included our memories of our first meeting. In 2008, I did not receive a Christmas card from Maureen, but did get an e-mail from her daughter telling me that Maureen had passed away. Her daughter related that she often heard the story of Jim and her mother.

Opt Out Vs. Opt In

Several cruise lines with ships that carry fewer than four hundred passengers also have dance hosts—normally two. As a result everyone gets to know everyone else pretty quickly, which is good. Among the guests aboard one particular cruise like this were four gay gentlemen traveling as couples. This is not unique on cruises nowadays and, in fact, I see more and more gay and lesbian couples sailing.

It is customary for us not to ask any lady to dance who is accompanied by a man. The reasons for this are obvious enough. The exception is if a gentleman specifically asks us to dance with his lady. So on one particular evening, the gay gentlemen were having a lot of fun—so much so that several adjoining couples prevailed upon the cruise director to settle them down. A waiter we knew well told us that one of the gentlemen was goading his partner into requesting a dance from one of us. Now I try to be broad-minded about people's choice of lifestyles, but I couldn't imagine one of these gentlemen approaching a male passenger with that request. I was prepared to suffer the consequences of turning down an invitation to dance from one of these men. I told my colleague Jack, and he agreed that we would stick together. As it turned out, we never had to do anything because none of these gentlemen asked, but it did remind me that times they are changing, and even hosts need to be mindful of that.

A year later I was on another ship and had a lesbian couple for table companions. Also at the table was a gentleman from California and another from England, plus a lady from Nevada and a very gracious woman from England, who I knew from previous cruises. Did I mention that a Catholic priest was also with us? I had not yet discerned that two of the ladies were partners when I put my foot in my mouth big time. During a lull in the conversation, I announced that after dinner tomorrow evening there would be a get-acquainted party for people traveling alone and I hoped to see all of them there. With that, the feminine half of the lesbian couple said they were partners, so she guessed they couldn't come. Without dropping a beat, I said, "You are guests at my dining table, and of course you are invited." This couple could not have been more friendly and interesting, and their behavior should have been a model for some other passengers.

Next evening, at the party, everyone from my table was present. (Maybe it was the free cocktails.) At one point, I saw the lesbian couple dancing. It seemed the most natural thing to me. As they exited the floor, one of them asked me if I was going to dance with her. We did, and as we walked from the floor, I complimented her partner on her dancing and offered to shake hands. That offer was graciously accepted.

I thought afterward, why my difference of attitude in these two situations? Did my behavior make sense in either or both of these cases? Here is what I concluded: My whole life had been immersed in conservatism. Family values, respect for others, and learning how to win and lose graciously was the norm in my family. I never had to make many decisions about social mores since they were part of my upbringing. Gay meant happy. Queer meant odd. Lesbian was a term I didn't hear, let alone fully understand, until well into my thirties. With changes in social behaviors came my change in attitude. Some came easily; others changes were more difficult. In every case, I tempered those changes with tried and true feelings I had always possessed. After much soul searching, I concluded that for better or worse, I would have handled these two situations exactly the way I did originally. If either or both were wrong, then so be it.

Don't Believe Everything You Read

I n March 2010, my ship stopped at Bandar Abbas, Iran, population 375,000. I was told it was the first time a cruise ship had stopped at this port in Iran. Since we were there for just the day, I signed up for a bus tour so I could see as much of the town as possible. I was aware that the US had sanctions against Iran based on political and ideological factors, and I wanted to see how actually being there would affect my feelings toward Iran and its people.

Our guide was a young lady who could have been a beauty pageant contestant. Dark flashing eyes could not hold back an equally flashing smile. Her British accent hinted at an overseas education. She was articulate and friendly and did her job efficiently and accurately. About one hundred fifty passengers were on the tour, divided among five buses. Each bus had three security persons aboard, a guide, a footman, and the driver. Also, a police car escorted each bus as it drove through the city. At each intersection, the police car would stop traffic so our buses could proceed unimpeded. I later learned that Iran is trying hard to develop a tourism business.

A short stop at the Anthropological Museum located in an old Hindu Temple gave me a flavor of the history of the Persian Empire. The artifacts and information from this civilization that had ruled the Near East for centuries seemed to stand in stark contrast to my impression of the new Iran and its current regime.

Next were the ancient baths of the city. Although inoperative, our guide related their history and their significance to the people of the Persian Empire. In ancient days the baths served as a meeting place for government leaders to discuss policy.

A scheduled stop at an open market close to the seaside turned out to be most remarkable. The fruits and vegetables were huge, the greens looked fresh and abundant, and the shoppers scurried among the stalls to select the choicest of the choice. The fish market adjoined the open market. I learned quickly that these two were the center of daily activity for many Iranians. I climbed the steps to the fish market entrance. My bus mates held back a little, no doubt in deference to the impression we get from our media of the political differences between Iran and the West. Armed with the fact that I had at least three security persons nearby, I was not about to miss this opportunity.

I walked into the fish market and was immediately struck by its cleanliness and minimal odor. The seafood was neatly arranged in ice-laden trays. The shrimp were larger than I had ever seen, the crab was monstrous—Bandar Abbas is nicknamed the Crab Port—and the vendors seemed friendly. As I looked around, I found myself eye-to-eye with a bearded man who was with his black-robed wife. Her burka left only her eyes exposed. She was carrying plastic bags and was two paces behind him. Neither of us broke eye contact. He smiled. After several seconds, I approached him as he shuffled forward toward me. My guess was he was in his early seventies. He pointed to me and said, "American?" I nodded yes. I then said to him, as I pointed, "Iranian?' He nodded and burst out laughing. I thought to myself, "Duh what else?" I pointed to myself and said, "James." He pointed to himself and said, "Farad." He did not introduce his wife. I glanced at her occasionally, but each time she averted her eyes. Not knowing what else to say to Farad, I offered my hand. He shook it enthusiastically. He then smiled from ear to ear as he looked around the market to ensure that those he knew (and those he didn't) were sure to see his encounter with an American. I finally detached myself from his grip, smiled, bowed slightly, and then turned away. The pleased look in his eyes as I gave him a quick pat on the shoulder told me I was not out of line. In part, my abrupt departure was to hide the lump in my throat. As I walked away a few yards, I glanced back over my shoulder. Farad stood there, a little taller than I first judged him to be, and we exchanged a last smile and a wave. His wife's head was averted. One day I will return to Iran. I hope I will meet more Farads. I looked up that name and it means "Unique." Most times around the world, I have found you get what you give, and this was no exception.

NORTHERN STAR

On an early 2005 cruise from Los Angeles to Papeete, Tahiti, I met Ian, a writer for a large Canadian newspaper. It turned out he was aboard with his wife, Colleen, as guests of the VP of Marketing for the cruise line. I was an onboard dance host. He was writing an article about the trip. Someone had suggested he chat with me about the duties and responsibilities of my position. In a brief interview, I explained to him that my job was to dance with unescorted ladies at several venues every evening. Additionally, I told this very proper gentleman that I host a table at dinner, and volunteer to escort occasional land tours. I elaborated that as one gains experience in my position it becomes clear that when you're not in your cabin, "You're on!" I told him that guests frequently ask us hosts, who wear name badges, all kinds of questions, and that we try to resolve every one or find someone who can.

Later that evening, I was surprised when Ian and Colleen chose seats near the dance floor. I smiled at them both, acknowledging their presence. On a hunch, I asked Ian if his wife would care to dance. With smiles, they both accepted my invitation, and I escorted her to the floor. I had previously explained that we hosts don't generally dance with escorted ladies unless their husbands request it, but in this case I felt it would add to his understanding of the role we play. This most enchanting lady of Irish heritage was an accomplished dancer, and I kept her to a nearby part of the floor so Ian could watch. Imagine my surprise when on one turn I saw him photographing us. By my count he must have taken six or more pictures. I was flattered, and I wondered if one of these photos would make it into the article.

Over the next several days, I bumped into Ian and Colleen around the ship while he was interviewing colleagues and passengers. They seemed to be enjoying their cruise and collecting a lot of information. On a port day in Raiatea, in the New Society Islands, two of my host buddies and I were strolling through town to see what we could see, when it started to rain. We sought out a café and, lo and behold, here was my new favorite couple. They asked us to join them, and for the next hour over beers we answered Ian's careful and non-threatening questions and shared experiences we had had as hosts over the years. I took a couple of pictures. It was now my turn.

On the final evening of the cruise, Ian and Colleen showed up at one of our venues, and she indicated to me that she would like to dance. We had two dances that evening, and I could not tell whose smile was broader, hers for dancing, his for having her dance, or mine for seeing them have such fun. They left the ship after thirteen days in Papeete. Though I didn't get to say goodbye to them, I did receive a wonderful note in my cabin. Ian thanked me for giving him a good start on his article. He enclosed his business card with his e-mail address. Later I e-mailed him the pictures I had taken. As I hit the send button, I wondered if Ian would send me a copy of the article he had written. He never did. Nevertheless it confirms why I do hosting on the seas. It is the people you meet more than the places you visit, or the payback you might get, that add to my feelings of well-being and warmth.

CELL PHONES

Since the global use of cell phones has grown, I have gotten used to seeing people on them in many circumstances. Using them while driving, while pushing a shopping cart, or while jogging are several of the routine sights I see often at home. In Hong Kong, nearly every other person is on a cell phone while walking to and from work because they seem to be as plentiful as cigarettes. A friend of mine told me of seeing a lady in Mumbai, India, begging with one hand while she was talking on a cell phone with the other. Talk about bad for business!

During one trip, I dined at a very upscale restaurant located on Sydney Harbour, in Australia, and I sought out the facilities. In the men's restroom was a well-dressed gentleman relieving himself with the stall door open. In his left hand he held a cell phone and carried on a loud and animated conversation as his noisy stream accompanied his voice. I couldn't help but imagine how funny it would have been if the party on the other end was likewise postured. Or if the party on the other end was icing a cake, or browsing through a copy of an adventure magazine. I wondered also if he would end his conversation just as the last drop splashed into the bowl. I didn't stay long enough to find out. I'm sure he would have at least had to interrupt his conversation to shake and zip.

CAMERON

Cameron was a brand new dance host and boarded a cruise ship in Miami, Florida, in October 2008, for the first of a three-cruise assignment in the Caribbean. I met him the first day, and we had lunch together. Our placement agent had told him to look me up and that I could answer any questions he might have about being a dance host. I felt honored that the placement agency thought highly enough of me to recommend newer hosts seek me out. On the other hand, I am very cautious about giving advice to someone I have just met. I don't want to take on the responsibility for behaviors they may bring with them, nor do I want to leave the impression that I am a lead host. My standard reply for any new guy is to follow the published daily schedule as it applies, and if he has any specific questions I would be glad to help. Other than that I merely say, "Being a dance host is not difficult if you apply the social behaviors your parents taught you as you were growing up and use some common sense." I always add that we all must read the published dance host guidelines of "do's and don'ts" provided by our agent and comply with them.

Cameron continued to show up late, if at all, for our scheduled dance sets. When he did come, he was a pretty good dancer unless the band was playing a rumba, cha-cha, waltz, foxtrot, samba, mambo, or swing number. His idea of daytime "country club casual" dress was a crew neck T-shirt complete with an advertisement of his favorite watering hole back home emblazoned across the back. I must admit it complemented his faded blue jeans perfectly. The sockless scuffed loafers also provided a nice touch. He more than made up for this when he appeared in a white dinner jacket on formal night when the schedule called for a black tux. I guess we three other hosts missed the change in instructions along with the cruise director and his staff. I was told that the dining table he was to host had "unrequested" his presence, and he ended up eating at a special table for one. When he spoke, which was constantly, his brain was unencumbered by very much knowledge.

What I failed to realize was that not all parents had the same idea of what appropriate social behaviors are. Also, I gave Cameron more credit than he deserved when it came to using common sense. He must have received an updated set of guidelines, because most of his actions were certainly not outlined in the guidelines I received from our agent. I felt no overpowering need to step in and offer him comments. Presumably he went through the same interview process and dance evaluation that I did.

I'm sure the paying guests were really upset when the cruise line elected to cut short his contract from the original thirty-six days to twelve days so he could return home early. I know I was.

PAULINE

Sail-a-ways on a cruise ship are really a lot of fun and exhilarating. The passengers are all agog with their new found home away from home and there is a feeling of adventure as they pull away from the dock waving at friends, real and imagined. Additionally, it is an ideal time for the cruise director, his staff, and we hosts to brush elbows for the first time with the newly embarked passengers. It is against this background that I approached Pauline who was standing by herself away from the masses on the promenade deck, and introduced myself.

This five-foot package of dynamite from British Columbia looked me straight in the eye and said, "If you're one of those guys who get paid to dance with widows, then I really don't want to talk to you, or for that matter have anything to do with you." I resisted the temptation to tell her not to hold back, let it all out. I composed myself and said, "I have no idea where you got the perception about hosts that you have, but if you would just give me five minutes to explain briefly what we are and what we are not, I will then honor your request if that's what you want."

I accepted her silence as a signal to talk, and for the next several moments gave her some real basics about hosts and hosting. I told her that hosts are not paid. Hosts do what they do because it is a fun way to see the world and meet new people. We love to dance and yes, we dance with any unescorted lady who would care to dance. We act as dance partners in dance classes aboard for those wanting the same. We host a dinner table to provide companionship and conversation to unescorted ladies. We treat all persons with respect and courtesy. Hosts do not target one lady of their or her choice for extra special or intimate treatment. Hosts are a valuable asset to help ensure all passengers, particularly unescorted ladies, have a pleasant cruise experience.

Pauline smiled slightly and excused herself saying, "Perhaps we could discuss this further later. I have some questions to ask you." I said I would welcome that opportunity, but it would be her call. At the first chance I got, I related my experience to my friend Mike, another host. He said he would be on the lookout for the lady and try to assist in allaying her misgivings regarding hosts.

Over the next couple of days, both Mike and I engaged Pauline in conversation, and by the third day we were both dancing with her several times each evening. She was a delightful lady, recently widowed, and determined to seek fullness for herself in her new life. By the end of the cruise, Pauline was a regular at all dance classes and evening dance sets. She had made some new female friends and was a most interesting and contributing dinner companion. Mike and I agreed at cruise end that just maybe, Pauline had a wonderful time dancing and socializing with us six hosts.

A postscript to this is that shortly after I returned to my home from the ship, I received a letter from Pauline. She included a copy of a letter to the president of the cruise line in question extolling his host program in general and specifically two fine gentlemen,

Jim and Mike, without whom she would have been utterly at a loss. About one year later, I met Pauline on another cruise. She asked if I remembered her. How could I not remember this lady? She delighted in relating, to anyone who would listen, the story of our first meeting. She hardly missed a dance on this cruise. I have had fleeting thoughts that my encounter with Pauline was part of a well-planned and executed ploy. Naw, she wouldn't…or would she?

What's A Host To Do?

What happens when a particular lady tries to monopolize a host's time? On one hand, we must be approachable and attentive, but on the other, doing so may send the wrong message and may lead her to believe that she's found Mister Right. After all, a cruise is a glamorous adventure and provides the perfect environment for romance.

A host might be affected the same way. He might love to concentrate his attention on one certain lady and monopolize her time. He may even get a come-hither signal from the object of his intended affection. He then is faced with the duty versus desire dilemma. I have personally witnessed both of these scenarios among lady passengers and fellow hosts. To be honest, I have found myself in the same dilemma.

Although ladies may be aware of the "equal attention rule," they are under no obligation to play it that way. There is no penalty, except perhaps a bruised ego, for pursuing their goal.

The host, on the other hand, has a great deal to lose. Succumbing in either case will cost him dearly. At best, he will incur the wrath of his fellow hosts and the remaining unescorted ladies. At worst, he may be asked by the cruise director to leave the ship at the next port for violating his contract, written or verbal. Either way, it's a lose-lose proposition for the host.

A cruise ship, regardless of its size, is like a little town. Nothing happens that isn't noticed by someone. There is a saying that if someone sneezes on the Lido Deck, the whole ship catches a cold. Rumors fly and perceptions often get more attention than facts. Hosts are at or near the center of cruise activities, so it is not unusual for them to see what is going on. An experienced host can spot an adventurous single lady or an overly attentive host in no time. Why should he care? First, if one out of, say, six hosts is concentrating his time on one or two ladies, it throws an additional burden on the remaining hosts. Some lady who wants to dance is going to be left out, and that's not fair or smart. Secondly, if a lady is creating an uncomfortable position for a host, his counterparts can help defuse or eliminate the situation. After all, we were presumably chosen as hosts, in part, because of our people skills.

So what is a host to do? It's pretty simple. Don't initiate a special relationship with a lady that could lead to a problem. Don't encourage a lady passenger who has displayed a special interest in you. Explain the hosting rule if that becomes necessary. Rely on your fellow host's observations and intuitions. Seek their opinions on all iffy situations. The group is a team, and everyone should support one another. If, after all your efforts to defuse a lady's advance (or to repress your desire) fails, get her e-mail and telephone number and promise to get in touch after the cruise. Some hosts who have done that were rewarded with a lifelong partner. At the very least, you may succeed in establishing a new friendship, as I have. Now that I have preached the party line, let me tell you about three of the ladies I've seen off the ship. Others have died or moved on and, sadly, we no longer keep in touch.

LaRue of Denver, Colorado, was an educational professional who asked me to escort her on a four-day getaway in Aspen. We joined three couples who were her close friends. Our unforgettable whirlwind of touring and partying left me breathless. Since 1991 we have exchanged greeting cards and, up until a couple of years ago when she remarried, she was on my Christmas morning telephone call list.

Gail, hailing from Springville, Alabama, really got me interested during a 1992 cruise to Greece. She was a real southern beauty who oozed charm, class, and tradition. I had more than a passing interest in her, and I knew she knew it. Unfortunately, the North versus South was the trump card. We both laughed when she said her aunt told her prior to my first visit, "Don't show him your house; he will want to move in." I visited several times after that, and we remained close telephone friends.

Marlene, a divorcee, who I had met in early 1993 on a cruise in the Caribbean, was a native of Stockton, California. When she was in Philadelphia at a convention, she asked if I would like to meet her for a big gala that was the windup event. I did, and we had a great evening. Since her return flight ticket was open-ended, I asked if she would like to visit my home. We spent four beautiful days touring the Amish country, New Hope, PA, and the resorts of the Pocono Mountains. Several years ago, Marlene remarried her former husband. We still are in touch after nineteen years. Good for her.

WE HEAR THE WHOLE DEAL

The name badge that we hosts wear is, I believe, a license to steal. While I'm wearing it, I can easily approach anybody and legitimately engage them in conversation. That includes couples, singles, ladies, gentleman, children, crew, staff, entertainers, presenters, even celebrities. This is raw personal power beyond belief. In fairness, I must say that all staff and most crew on the ships I have been on wear name badges of one kind or another. Having a name tag makes our "hosting" much easier. Being a successful host requires meeting people quickly and getting them to feel comfortable. A gentleman without identification might find single ladies reluctant to talk or dance.

As the cruise progresses and the unescorted ladies get to know you as a host, interesting things can happen. The ladies recognize that the chance of them seeing you again after the cruise end is remote. Thus, they will share information with you they normally would keep private. The following is a sampling of some things I've I have been told by passengers.

Linda, a real looker from Salt Lake City, confided in me that the guy she was traveling with and sharing accommodations with was gay. So she could hang out with dance hosts and other single guys without fear of retribution. Unwanted attention in the living quarters was not a problem, of course.

Jane, a tall blonde from Minnesota, told me with tears in her eyes how she came on this cruise to make her boyfriend jealous. It wasn't working because she was having a miserable time because of her guilt over her childish behavior.

John, from New York City, confided that his wife told him that if they couldn't get it together on this cruise, she was kissing him off as soon as they got home. He added that no matter what he did, it seemed to be wrong. He had accepted he would be wifeless soon after they disembarked.

Myra from Louisiana, offered that she had a real thing for one of the officers and would make sure he was aboard before she booked her next cruise. Thereafter, I noticed her with him during his lunch and other off-duty hours.

One lady asked me not to dance too closely with her. She was reserving that privilege for one of my host colleagues. Thereafter, I chose her only when a swing, samba, or cha-cha was played.

Louise, a raven-haired serious woman, came aboard because a particular host was on. She and he had been keeping steady company for about six years, she confessed. But about one month before the start of this cruise, he had broken up with her. She was aboard to try to rekindle the flame. Watching him try to dodge her, yet still do his job, was entertaining.

In all cases, these people just wanted to vent a little. They weren't looking for me to solve their problem but to just listen to their plight. I learned a willing ear is as good, maybe better, than a helpful hand.

TAKING THE "U" OUT OF ARGUE

Asuper cruise in the Baltic Sea area visiting wonderful ports and capitals yielded this little example of human behavior and how location or situation can change it. From the start of this cruise, I wondered why George and Sarah from New Hampshire were here. Nothing was right—the food, the crew, the shows, the casino. Nothing pleased them, including each other. Abusive is mild for the way they vented at each other. He dressed like a "farmer," she admonished. Her family were freeloaders, he exhorted. His mother had four legs and lived under her porch. On and on it went for several days.

At Warnemunde, Germany, the ship made a stop, and many of the passengers took a day trip by train to Berlin. I was assisting the tour manager by helping direct passengers the several hundred yards from the ship to the train station. I could see George and Sarah coming down the gangplank. I cringed to think I would be spending the rest of the day with or around them. It was with great surprise that I watched them pass by holding hands and smiling. You couldn't have pried them apart with a crowbar. I was on the same train car and later the same bus as my favorite couple was. Something was very wrong here. These love doves could not have been more considerate of others or themselves throughout most of the whole trip. At one point they became separated by about fifteen feet at a check point near the Berlin Wall. The look of panic on Sarah's face faded when I escorted her five steps to an equally panicked George. She promptly locked her arm in his as they continued on the tour.

I was convinced that a miracle had happened right here at the entrance of the Iron Curtain. At day's end, Sarah and George strolled, again hand-in-hand, from the train to the ship's gangway. They smiled as they boarded, and I was really looking forward to getting to know them better on the rest of the trip. However, in no time, Sarah and George were back to their old ways of mutual insulting. I shrugged and made a mental note to pay attention to more happy people.

Our next stop, St. Petersburg, Russia, found George and Sarah once again entwined as they quietly enjoyed the sights of this marvelous city. I finally realized that whenever they were feeling uncomfortable in unfamiliar territory, they put aside their differences to provide mutual protection from the unknown. When they were once again in a safe environment, they resumed their mutual torture treatment. It was a classic example of what psychologists call the "fulfillment of needs" theory. I entertained the idea of transplanting George and Sarah into a group of headhunters somewhere.

THE BELLWETHER

Dance hosts are, on occasion, also asked to serve as tour escorts. All cruise lines I have been on offer land tours for passengers on days that the ship is in port. These consist of an expert guide plus someone from the cruise line staff. The procedure makes perfect sense. An escort acts as a liaison between the shore side tour guide and the passengers. Also included among the tour escort's duties is the following: Assist handicapped persons with negotiating steps, traffic, and so on; make sure everybody is back on the bus before it departs for the next leg of the tour; be the recognizable "tie" between the ship and the passengers; assist with minor problems if they arise. All in all, it is a great experience, especially because in return for being an escort you get to take the tour for free.

Since each tour group consist of roughly thirty-five people, it is not unusual for four to six groups of passengers to be covering the same tour route on foot at roughly the same time. By far the biggest challenge is to keep track of your "thirty-five people" and make sure no one gets lost or separated from his or her assigned group. This is not an easy chore in places like the Great Wall of China, the Sistine Chapel, or the Hermitage. One late or lost person at bus departure time can cause hostility among the rest of the group since no one likes delays. In extreme cases it can delay the ship sailing, which is critical.

I have been an escort about four hundred times over the years and am always nervous about keeping track of my flock. Sometimes the professional guide outdistances the group or makes a quick turn around a corner and has the instant challenge of corralling everyone. I always look disdainfully on the inevitable one or two people who have to stop to gaze into a shop window or look at some statue. Inevitably, they are the ones who turn up missing when it is time to board the bus. I once had a lady who stopped to visit with a local person to inquire of a relative who she believed lived in this town. I also had a gentleman who just decided he would skip the church visit and do a little shopping. One time, a couple decided to enjoy an unscheduled coffee break.

On all three of these occasions, I had to find them and "reacquaint" them with the others.

Logistically, the tour guide leads the way carrying an identifying sign, usually a number, for the group. Ideally, everyone keeps pace and there is no problem. A tour escort will bring up the rear, ensure that everyone is on the right path, and count heads. Up until recently, I never found a good way of assuring myself that all members of the group were with us. Making a head count of a moving group is not the easiest thing to do. It is my job to hold the guide up until the whole group is present and ready to proceed. I have noticed over the years that in any one group it is always the same person or persons who are the stragglers. I give this no special thought other than to vent my unspoken "praises" upon them time and time again. In this case, I decided to forget about the rest of the group and identify who the laggard was. I figured I could be pretty sure that if I saw him in or near the group, I probably had everyone. That reasoning sounds a little oblique, but it works. In fact I have coined the term "The Bellwethers" for these people.

So on every escort assignment I get, I identify the bellwether(s) and keep track of him/her/them, and the rest of the group takes care of itself with minimal attention from me. Since employing this method, I get to enjoy the tours a lot more than I have in the past. Another very interesting and wonderful thing has happened. The person(s) who I previously viewed with disdain because of their tardiness have become a sort of welcome sight to me, and I have showered attention upon them and found out they were really very nice and interesting people.

FACE TIME

The bauble that hung around her neck was a diamond that seemed as large as a quail egg. It was the Captain's Welcome Night party aboard a cruise ship in the waters off Acapulco, Mexico, and I was dancing with Simone, a beautiful lady from Newport Beach, California. Though admitting to being "over sixty," she looked mid forties. Her slim figure was topped with a generous bosom, and her flashing smile lit up the room. Her clothes had to come from the most chic of ladies' boutiques, and they fit her just right. Everyone gaped at her. Well-managed blond tresses hung to her shoulders, and well-manicured nails completed the picture. The smile she occasionally flashed as we danced made me indeed feel special. But as we danced, no matter where I turned, her face was always away from the band and toward the room and its occupants. Now the challenge of exploring my theory took over. No matter what dance move I created to turn her toward the band, somehow she managed to at least have a profile, if not a full face, to the crowd. I was a firsthand witness and accomplice to the art of "managed exposure" performed better than any politician could hope for. My suspicions of her attention-getting prowess were confirmed when I was approached by at least five people later that evening inquiring, "Who was that beauty you were dancing with?"

"A very close friend." I told them.

Supervision By Splattering Blame

Among the not-so-wonderful experiences that hosts endure include being called on the carpet by a supervisor when something is not going well. Complaints may be legitimate for inappropriate behavior, or they may be bogus for a perceived breaking of the rules and guidelines we hosts ascribe to. Infractions (real or perceived) could include dancing too closely with a lady, bestowing too much attention on one lady, not dancing with all the ladies, using sexually suggestive language, and over-consumption of alcoholic beverages. I can truthfully say that rarely are the alleged violations as serious as they are portrayed by guests, but for the sake of this story let us assume that someone has indeed been slighted or embarrassed by a host.

The normal course of events would result in the complaint being filed with the cruise director. If the complaint centered on the dance venue, it would be the responsibility of the dance instructor to deal with it. This makes sense because many cruise lines rely on the dance instructors to monitor the host schedules and their performance. By this time, most hosts would already know or at least suspect that something was amiss. Secrets don't last long on ships.

Given the choice between privately approaching the "errant" host, explaining the complaint and seeking resolution, or calling a meeting of all hosts for that purpose, the latter is usually chosen. This defuses the specifics of the "crime" since the supervisor will usually not identify the host being targeted, the complainant, or the circumstances surrounding the incident. It becomes a broad-brush accusation, and no host really knows who is being singled out or who has been slighted. The natural reaction by the innocent and the presumed guilty is, "Are they talking about me? I haven't done anything wrong; what is this all about? Who is complaining?" Then the supervisor ends by saying something like, "We all need to be careful, we all are adults, and we know certain people are sensitive, and we need to be aware that even the slightest infraction is taken seriously by our guests. As the meeting ends, all we hosts know is that someone did something to someone, and whatever it was shall cease by whoever did it to whomever. We leave with our own thoughts. The old adage, "When the crap hits the fan, it is rarely distributed evenly" has been proven to be wrong. It has been distributed evenly among us hosts, the guilty, the innocent, and the baffled.

PUTTING ON THE DOG

They came aboard for an Alaskan cruise as a party of five: grandfather, his daughter and son-in-law, and their two small children. The kids were boys, one seven and the other four. Their parents I judged to be in their mid-thirties. The grandfather appeared to be sixty-five going on thirteen. His name was John, and indeed he marched to a different drummer. He was an over-weight man of medium height with a goatee badly in need of a trim. Though I never really met him, I observed him often on this ten-day cruise. Everywhere he went, he carried a dog—a small, black, fuzzy thing that sat cuddled in the crook of his left arm. He would stroke it with his right hand, and its head would move up and down in a very cute fashion. Of course, the "dog" really was a puppet, whose movements John controlled.

Everywhere John went, so did his "dog," including breakfast, lunch, and even in the formal dining room. Since it looked so realistic, people would wonder how a dog was allowed on the ship.

John would go into his overly loud act demonstrating how cute he thought his dog was and tell long stories to his audience. This made him feel like a king and his inquirer like cold toast. John would roam the decks at all hours, with or without his grandsons, just begging to be asked about his dog. Toward the end of the cruise, people actually started avoiding him when he was out and about on his quest for attention. John's daughter and son-in-law totally ignored him, too. Unfortunately, the grandsons and passengers had a hard time doing the same. Though my initial reaction to John and his behavior was very negative, I ended up feeling sorry for this guy who seemed not to be able to command anyone's attention through the normal communication channels.

WHEN SECOND COMES FIRST

On a recent cruise out of Hawaii to the South Seas, I was having breakfast with two widows. As a couple passed by, I heard one remark to the other "Second." Her friend nodded knowingly. I inquired as to the meaning of this secret exchange, and they both chuckled. They explained that they enjoyed trying to guess whether a couple was in their first marriage or the "second time around" category. They added that when a gentleman takes a second wife he will invariably begin holding doors, pulling out chairs, buying the best wines, dressing up for dinner, fetching drinks from the bar, and even dancing. Their pastime intrigued me. They confided that most of the time it was a no brainer. For instance, one of the ladies said that for her entire married life of forty-eight years she somehow always seemed to be two paces behind her husband wherever they went. She told him that if she died first and looked down to see him walking side-by-side with a new bride that she would surely return to Earth and create a living hell for him. I believe she meant it. I began to check out the "second marriage" theory, and I must say the ladies had it right. I noticed particularly that newer pairs seem to hold on to each other most of the time. Recently, on a long cruise, I actually saw a couple holding hands while jogging. Or maybe they were just jogging as they held hands. Either way, they were definitely "seconds."

WHAT A DEAL/SHAME

S he was an attractive eighty-year-old lady from somewhere in the Southern United States—well-spoken, well-dressed, and obviously financially well off. Cruising with her was her son and daughter-in-law. Nightly, I would see them in the lounge having a pre-dinner cocktail, but later they would eat early and catch the early show. Later I would see Elvira alone at the dancing venues. She preferred to waltz, and I would try to dance with her early in the set. After one or two dances, she would disappear until the next evening. I would see the son and daughter-in-law throughout the day but never Elvira.

This routine continued throughout the cruise. Although I'd exchange a few words with the son from time to time, I really didn't give them much thought until they turned up on the next cruise. Sure enough, Elvira resumed her routine. Around the third or fourth night out, her son, Wallace, approached me and asked if I would join him for a drink. We settled down in the lounge, and he asked if I would be on for the next cruise. I said no, that my three-cruise assignment would be up, and I'd be going home. He smiled and then asked if I'd be willing to stay for another cruise to look after his mother. He would pay for my stateroom and any onboard expenses in exchange for escorting her for cocktails, dinner, the early show, and maybe one or two dances. Other than that my time would be my own, whether at sea or in port. He said his sister and her husband would be joining the ship after that and I could then return home. I said I would think about it and get back to him.

The next day, I happened to run into Wallace's wife, June. She took me aside and told me that Elvira was very needy. She said they hardly had any time to themselves at home so they were happy to see her stay aboard. That sent up a red flag and changed my mind from "maybe" to "most certainly not." I saw Wallace the next morning and thanked him for the offer, but declined, fibbing that getting home was a priority for me. Later that day one of my colleagues, Carson, who also was to disembark to go home, spotted me and related this fabulous deal that a guy named Wallace had offered him. I said nothing.

I left the ship and had been home about three days when the first of several e-mails arrived from Carson. Now it appeared that Elvira wanted to be escorted off the ship on port days. She would buy two tickets for an excursion, and Carson now had an additional chore. Plus, the pre-dinner cocktail time was being stretched to its limit. Dinner was at a table for two and went on so long they often missed the early show. So the "one or two" dance thing had become the whole set, so they could then catch the second show. After that, a post-show cocktail was in order before Carson finally escorted Elvira to her stateroom around midnight. When he had balked at the deal, Elvira reminded him that she could always speak to the cruise director about his failure to live up to her understanding of the agreement. Being a dance host, this could jeopardize future assignments.

Poor Carson could hardly wait for the twelve-day cruise to end so he could go home to rest.

PANCAKES

It was a beautiful day in Tallinn, Estonia. Fellow host Phil and I caught the shuttle bus from the ship to this little town on the Baltic Sea. We got a map and started our exploration about 9:30 a.m. With directions from a local, we found Old Town and walked onward. We passed many churches as we strode the cobblestone streets. Window-shopping gave us a flavor of what was available to buy. The local people looked well scrubbed and energetic as they sped off to their appointments of the day. We peeked in a few of the ornate Russian Orthodox Churches and one modest Lutheran Church. Around 11:00 a.m. we decided to have beer at an outdoor café and people watch. The hostess ushered us to a pleasant curbside table, and each of us ordered Sava, the local beer. I chose a dark one for about three dollars. As we sipped, we chatted with the young hostess, who spoke some English. Phil asked her what kind of food is popular in Estonia. She said they had all kinds of food and offered us a menu. This turned out to be an Italian café, so pizza and pasta were prevalent, but that wasn't what we had in mind. We tried asking for some local cuisine, but the hostess didn't understand, and we finally gave up. A lady who had been sitting next to us rose to leave and stopped by our table to say she had overheard the conversation and recommended we try the pancakes, which were truly local fare. She went on to describe how you could get pancakes with a variety of fillings, and that that was real Estonian food. We thanked her, finished our beer, paid the bill, and left. On our walk, we ran into some people from the ship, and Phil told them about the pancakes. I finally said to Phil, "I don't care if it's noon; let's find pancakes." We stopped at one place, but they didn't serve them. But I was determined to find these illusive pancakes. I asked at another restaurant, and it also did not serve them, but the waiter directed us to a place he thought did. "Up two blocks and over one," he said. We followed the directions and found a restaurant named Kompressor. It was a drab place with large windows on a narrow but clean street. It looked totally empty. We entered anyway, found a young lady at the counter, and asked if they were open. When she nodded, I asked the crucial question: "Do you have pancakes?" She replied that they did and showed us a menu. The menu showed pancakes with a choice of sixteen different fillings. Not only could we get pancakes with fruit fillings or jam, but also pancakes stuffed with the likes of tuna, chicken, ham and cheese, trout, or beef. Phil chose the pancakes stuffed with shrimp. I opted for the ones with bacon and smoked cheese. The crepe-like pancakes were the size of a huge round placemat that had been folded over twice. It had to be at least one and a half inches thick in the center and was completely stuffed with filling. And it was delicious. No way could we finish them. Phil and I left fully satisfied with our Estonian food experience, and fully stuffed as well.

A WIN-WIN WITH WINNIE

Early in a cruise from Cape Town to Durban, South Africa, I noticed a group of eight ladies at one of our dance venues. They were obviously together, chatting and celebrating. Another host and I approached them and asked two of the ladies to dance. The apparent leader of the group accepted my invitation, and we took to the floor. It turned out she was a travel agent escorting a group of agents on a four-day familiarization trip (FAM trip). Cruise lines find that bringing a group of travel agents aboard for a few days to familiarize them with the ship and its amenities helps those same travel agents to sell cruises.

She indicated that there was a journalist aboard who was planning to write an article about the ship. She asked if I would be willing to be interviewed for an article to appear in a South African newspaper. I asked her to point out the journalist, and she nodded to the woman dancing with my fellow host, Ed. I said that would be fine, and we made arrangements to meet the next afternoon.

Since Ed had been dancing with her, I asked him to come along, too. I always welcome the chance to be interviewed. They all contribute to my personal fifteen minutes of fame.

A couple of days later, we met with Winnie. This South African was the daughter of English immigrants. Her short-cropped grey, perfectly coiffured hair projected all business. She was a recent widow, exploring her dream of writing and traveling. Her questions were complete, professional, and pointed. Her prodding for information was non-threatening; I felt like we were having an interesting conversation. She shared some of her background and experiences as we related our own. A half hour later, we left the interview with her promise to send us a copy of her article. She took our pictures, gave us her e-mail addresses, and thanked us for our time.

Ed and I had done several interviews over the years that ended up on the pressroom floor. So, though we were honored with the opportunity to tell our hosting story, we were prepared for that to be the end of it. I left the ship and flew home. After about two months, I was going through some paperwork and found the journalist's e-mail address. On a whim, I e-mailed her. I told her that it was a pleasure to meet her and though we hadn't heard anything further about the article we were pleased to assist her with her efforts. By return e-mail, I received a wonderful note from her with an attachment of the article she had written and published in a South African daily newspaper.

She had done a wonderful job, and we e-mailed back and forth for several days. On our last exchange she attached a copy of the same article, this time published in a South African travel magazine. We had two published articles about hosting! This was truly a win-win event in my golden years. And yet it's another example of how a new acquaintance can enrich one's life. In the big scheme of things, a single encounter is not earth-shattering, but how is a whole life built? One experience at a time, and that's why I never pass up an opportunity to spend some time with new people no matter where I find them.

No I In Team

Picture nine baseball players of varying ages, educations, agendas, cultures, hometowns, skill levels, and life experiences. Now imagine putting them together and within eight hours fielding a winning ball team. The chances of being successful would be very low. Though a little oblique, this was the situation when eight gentlemen were thrown together on a cruise ship and had to become a well-coordinated dance group on the very first night of the trip. It is a testament to the cruise lines, the dance hosts they choose, and the latitudes they afford these gentlemen that this situation succeeds. Of course, the process it is not without problems. If a host is not willing to relinquish some personal wants or needs in deference to the team, problems will brew. If one or more hosts don't pull their fair share of the work assignments, it won't be long until complaints surface.

To the credit of those hosts I've known in my twenty- three years on ocean liners, river boats, and land tours, I can truly say that problems created by individual gentlemen not performing their duties are minimal. However, when they arise they are never small or easy to cover up. The secret is to keep the guests from seeing conflicts while the offense is corrected. Just as important is to try to keep unusual host behaviors from the "suits," namely the cruise director and the dance instruction team. But this rarely works. Here a few excuses I've heard from hosts for being absent or late for a scheduled event and are correctable. These are minor infractions on the surface but definitely do not promote the team spirit most hosts strive for and will lead to an unhappy group of colleagues.

I got stuck in the elevator.

The cruise director sent me on a special assignment.

The wakeup call didn't come through.

The water in the shower shut off while I was soaped up.

I needed to see the doctor.

You didn't need me. (My all-time favorite)

I thought it was my turn for the night off.

I fell asleep at the movie.

I was invited by one of the ladies to dinner.

The tour I was on was late returning to the ship.

Most of the intolerable behaviors are listed in a host manual, so there is no question about what is expected. Additionally, seasoned hosts are always available to ask if there is any question about borderline behaviors. Violation of these written rules can result in removal from the ship or having no chance of being asked back for future assignments. In my years of experience, this has happened maybe seven times. Examples of these are:

Drinking alcohol in excess. (1 case) Allen was an affable fellow. He was jovial and a little loud, but not overly so. His reddish nose did not belie the fact that he had an occasional drink. It was to the point that it was noticeable and affected his performance. No interceding by my fellow hosts seemed to get through to him. His three-cruise assignment turned into one.

Over-fraternization with a guest, staff, or crew member. (4 cases) A few hosts just can't curb the male animal instinct, and it will bite them most every time. In each case the extra attention was pretty flagrant and noticeable. Two of the cases were with willing lady passengers, one case was with an onboard entertainer, and the last case was with a male crew member. The results were two cases of probation and two outright dismissals.

Use of drugs. (0 cases) Thankfully. This is a violation that will dispatch the offender from the ship immediately whether host, crew member, staff, or even guest.

Physical confrontation with anyone. (1 case) Jonathon was sharing a cabin with fellow host Carmine. From the get-go they were not hitting it off. It turned out that Jonathan was the culprit who occupied three-quarters of the cabin. Littering of clothing, uneaten food, and paperwork added to mayhem. After ignored attempts to set things straight, Carmine sought out the cruise director with his complaint. Upon being confronted to correct the situation, Jonathan got livid. Back in the cabin, Carmine received a split lip, and Jonathan got a free pass off the ship.

Bad mouthing the cruise line or its staff. (1 case)

I knew we were in for eventual trouble from the first night. Brad, a short-fused guy, seemed to be complaining about everything. The food, the ladies we danced with, and the late-night working hours were just a few of his tirades. He finally settled on the house dance band to vent his anger in earnest. I guess he figured he could browbeat this fine sextet from Manila, who played very danceable music and were nice guys to boot. Brad berated them at the end of most sets for the choice of music they played. At the end of the first of four cruises Brad was scheduled to be on, he left the ship. He related to us that it was his choice, but I doubt it.

All in all, not a bad record for making the guilty walk the proverbial plank!

SILENCE SPEAKS VOLUMES

I was excited to be escorting a tour In Honolulu to the site of the Japanese attack that began World War II, including the famous Arizona Battleship Memorial in Pearl Harbor. It began with my group being ushered into an auditorium for a short movie. Then we were led to a boat that took us to the memorial. Throughout the short voyage, silence was the order of the day. Once we arrived, a soft-spoken guide explained some of the points of interest and then turned everyone loose. Despite the fact that there were many other groups present, the silence was overwhelming. At the pre-arranged time, my group reassembled at the boat landing for the trip back. Everyone was still noticeably quiet. Thousands of people of all nationalities visit the memorial every year, and this sign of respect was prevalent.

On a stop in Hiroshima, Japan, a few years later, I escorted a tour to the museum near Ground Zero where the first atomic weapon was dropped. It depicts via graphic photos and descriptions the conquest of the Asian Pacific Rim by the Japanese from the mid-1930s. The majority of the visitors were Japanese, and their silence reminded me of my Arizona Memorial experience. I thought if I ever had a chance to see other similar sites I would hear the same thing. Indeed, when I later visited the American cemetery in Normandy, France, I was not disappointed. Here, the visitors were not only American but also European. Elderly men shuffled around looking for long-lost comrades. They would shake their heads, wipe away a few tears, and speak softly to their traveling companions.

My last opportunity to witness this hushed respect for fallen heroes was at the American and Japanese memorials to both armies' soldiers on Guadalcanal. Though much smaller sites, the silence was just as pronounced. Respect, it seems, has no boundaries, no allegiances, and need not be vocalized.

KISSING ANNIE

The rule to not dance with the same lady twice in a row is reasonable, since there are usually more women who wish to dance than there are hosts. Thus it is not unusual for a lady to sit out two, sometimes three, dances before she gets her chance. Most ladies are patient until one of their "sisters" tries to jump the line somehow.

Kissing Annie had a methodology for getting more than her share of dances. In fact, it almost assured her of getting every other dance. Annie was maybe five feet tall, about seventy years of age, and well-known throughout the cruising industry. Her name came from her insistence on delivering a little peck on your cheek after you danced with her. It was pretty harmless since Kissing Annie was not blessed with great looks or attractive physical proportions. But here was her plan: When not dancing she would hang around near the edge of the floor and attach herself, literally, to the coat-tails of a host who was escorting a lady back to her seat. From our point of view, the dance with a lady begins at her seat and ends there as well. That is just good manners.

As the host exited the floor with his lady, Annie would grab the hem of his sports coat or tux and follow him. In this way she would claim the next dance before the gentleman had a chance to select his next partner. The host was not about to embarrass himself or cause a problem by refusing, so Annie always got the next dance. The other ladies would complain, but there wasn't much we could do. The cruise director, who could have set Annie straight, would usually choose not to because she was a prominent person in the cruise industry.

I had a little more luck in not putting myself in this awkward opposition. I would make sure that near the end of a dance I was at least twenty feet from where I saw Annie lurking. I would delay leaving the floor slightly so that one or two hosts left before me. As a result Annie would latch on to one of them, and I would be free to escort my dancing partner back to her seat and invite another. To protect my method and not ignore Annie, I would make sure she got to attach herself to my coattails once per set.

TIPPING

Many employees on cruise lines rely on gratuities for part of their income. Most passengers know this and respond accordingly. Others, however, think tipping is purely discretionary and not expected. No cruise line that I have ever worked for has indicated dance hosts should expect or solicit tips. In my experience, it is a topic dance hosts rarely discuss. However, from time to time we do get gratuities at the end of a cruise. They are normally nominal, and mostly come from Asian ladies who want to express their appreciation for our efforts. Refusing to accept these gratuities would be bad manners and culturally inappropriate in my opinion, so I graciously accept and thank the donor. I usually offer my personal card to them as a memento of our time together.

Once in a while, ladies will ask us about tipping. I always explain that tipping is not expected, and it is our pleasure just to have the honor of dancing with them. On one such occasion, Trixi, a delightful new cruiser, who was with us at nearly every set, asked me what would be appropriate. I responded as I always did but she insisted. Besides me, there were three other dance hosts on the team, so she handed each one an envelope. Three of us thanked her, but when I talked to her later she was very upset. Apparently the fourth member of our group took great exception to being offered the tip and declined it. That's fine if that's how strongly he felt, but he went on to tell the lady he wasn't a gigolo and resented the implication that the tip conveyed.

An entirely different scenario occurred with one of our dancing partners named Romaine from Colorado. Though married and aboard with her husband, she was present for each dance set nightly and stayed until the last beat. Each evening her husband would escort her to the dance venue, stay for one dance or so and then leave. The other ladies noticed this and felt since Romaine had a husband she should not be getting the dancing attention that we were giving her. In deference to their complaints some of my colleagues would skip her once in a while. In murky situations such as this, I have learned to err on the conservative side, so I continued to dance with Romaine as if she were any other unmarried and unescorted lady.

A couple of the hosts noticed this and asked me why I was doing this. I told them that until the cruise director told me differently the opinion of these ladies mattered not. At cruise end, as she was leaving the last evening's dancing, Romaine handed each of us six hosts an envelope and thanked us for making her cruise memorable. I waited until I reached my cabin and opened the envelope to find a crisp one hundred-dollar bill and a very nice note from Romaine.

Wrong Even If You're Right

The tour started out bad and got worse. The group I was escorting was on the last of three buses to leave the port for an afternoon tour of nearby Puerto Monte, Chile. Buses 1 & 2 were spaced about five minutes apart, and we brought up the rear. The tour guide stopped at various sites around the city as my group became more and more restless. They weren't impressed or interested in the gorgeous cathedral, the beautiful fountains in the main plaza, or the Angelama Green Goods Market, and they were vocal about it. Clearly, these people just wanted to be on their own. The guide perceived this and cut her charges loose with the instructions that Bus 3 would be leaving at 4:45 p.m. and to be sure not to miss it. My flock took off, and as they did so, I reminded them of the bus number and the departure time.

I now had about one and a half hours of free time until I'd have to return to the bus stop and account for my thirty passengers. So I did some shopping, as is my practice wherever

I stop. I had some casual conversations with a few of the vendors and then finally found myself at Club Aleman, where I had a beer. Puerto Monte has a German heritage, and the Club Aleman attested to that. I ran into several people from my group sitting on the bench. When they saw me, they said they were ready to head back. We still had a half hour until the appointed departure time, but that did not deter them from insisting on leaving now. One guy said he and his wife would take one of the other buses back since those would be first to leave. Another two couples hailed a cab and sped off. I headed back to the bus knowing that things were in really bad shape. I expected to find my tour guide there and make a plan of action to handle this. But she was not there. She finally arrived about five minutes before departure time to a half-full bus of anxious people who were ready to go. By this time, one other bus had already left, and the other one was about to.

One gentleman stood up and yelled that his wife was missing but would be along shortly. After ten minutes, I suggested to him that perhaps she had taken another bus. He said no, she was at a little shop right across the street. Finally, laden with packages, she stumbled onto the bus to the derisive applause of the rest of the group. In a loud voice, she said to her husband, "You told me the wrong time to be back." Thankfully, the return ride back to the ship was only about ten minutes, and I was very happy to have this tour over. As I entered the ship, the tour manager signaled me to come to his office. The complaints about this tour had preceded me, so he wanted my explanation of the incidents. He listened patiently, smiled, and then offered this parting comment: "Sometimes you're wrong even when you're right."

LAZY, HAZY, AND CRAZY

J acquelyn and Ed seemed to be ill-matched from the moment I
first met them. They boarded the ship in Tilbury, England, for
a twelve-day cruise up the west coast of Norway and returning
to Dover, England, via Ireland and Scotland. She was southern
born and bred with not a hint of a blemish on her skin. No signs of
those sunny summer days common to her home state of Georgia. I
guessed that the wide-brimmed hat she wore accounted in part for
her flawless complexion. She carried herself quietly with elegance
and self-assurance that bespoke old money. On the other hand,
Ed was a good old boy with the build of a lumberjack and the pure
good looks of a matinee idol. I judged his accent to be Midwestern,
and his words flowed from a wide grin that he sported most of the
time. He was friendly, outgoing, and never at a loss for words.

Ed was an early riser, so we had coffee together most mornings well before Jacquelyn got started on her day. He shared
with me that this was his second marriage and Jacquelyn's third.

They had met on a vacation and had hit it off from the get-go and married pretty quickly after that. He offered that he did not learn a great deal about her family so he did not fully appreciate marrying into a family with a set of twenty-three-year-old twin sons and a twenty-year-old daughter. Though his new bride had warned him before their wedding, when he took up residence in her home some three years ago, he found out that the "children" commanded a great deal of their mother's time and financing. He didn't complain since part of the marriage deal was that Jacquelyn would handle that, he told me. With a good-natured sigh of acceptance, he told me he had a name for each of the offspring based on how he viewed their behavior within the family.

One of the twin boys he called "Lazy" since he had no job or even prospects of one and rose around noon expecting his mother to fix his meals, clean his room, and provide some spending money so he could jump in his car and take off for the day. He always appeared at mealtime in the evening, which he shoveled down near the TV, then sped off to spend the evening with friends.

The other of the twin boys Ed labeled "Hazy "since his mind seemed to be in another world most of the time. Asked a simple question, he would not hear it, ignore it, or blurt out some unrelated answer to an unasked question. He was content to stay home most of the time and tinker in the garage trying to invent some really wonderful gadget that would make him a fortune. A two-way conversation with him was nearly impossible.

The girl he dubbed "Crazy" because that's what she was, said Ed. Everything she did or touched was a big deal that demanded instant response from her mother. If she didn't understand or didn't agree with the feedback she got, she would fly into a snit that would last hours. Between tears and shouts, she normally got her way. Ed said, "She would cry over card tricks." A constant parade of her friends would traipse through the house day and night, feed off her poor behavior, and become less than pleasant houseguests.

As Ed vented his frustrations, I could not help but wonder why he would tolerate this situation. He said that Jacquelyn was his true love and because of that he would tolerate the "kids" so long as they two could get away for a little rest and recovery from time to time. After all, he said the behaviors the trio exhibited were not because of him, as far as he knew, and had been established and apparently accepted by their mother long before he entered the scene. I wanted to ask him if he had shared his pet names for the three with Jacquelyn, but decided I didn't want to hear the answer, either way.

Breaking Up

We hosts attend all the group dance classes conducted by the resident dance instructors in order to provide partners for those ladies without them. It is a fun and rewarding time since most of the ladies who come are new to dancing.

On one such occasion, several of the ladies were Asian. Most of them spoke some English. Mandy, the one I was dancing with was having a difficult time following the instructions and my lead. She was lively and animated in her every move, but the messages were just not getting through. I encouraged her, but her smiling face did not hide her frustration. After many stops and starts, she looked at me, laughed loudly, and uttered these forever- remembered words: "My feet will not obey."

Not one to give up, Mandy started coming to our evening dance sets. She was bubbly and laughed a lot and would break me up when I asked her to dance. As I presented my arm to escort her to the floor, I would look down at her feet and say, "Now please obey." As I escorted her back to her chair afterward, she would comment, "My feet and I enjoyed the dance."

CALL ME WHAT YOU CHOOSE

The name badge I wear when assigned as a dance host aboard ship clearly states "James Wood." Since I have been cruising a lot of years, in addition to the new people I meet, I run into guests, fellow dance hosts, and ship staff. I have noticed that those I have sailed with previously call me "Jim." That's fine with me for I take it as a compliment that they feel comfortable using my less formal name. From time to time, a guest will ask which name I prefer. I always reply that either is fine.

Recently, a fairly rigid German lady we dance with, Freda, who calls me James, took great exception to another lady who referred to me as Jim. I tried to explain that as far as I was concerned that was not a slight but a less formal name for me, and if the lady was comfortable calling me Jim that was fine. She just shook her head and walked off. Of course she continued to call me James. Jim, coming from her, would not have sounded right anyway.

A very attractive lady, Michele, from Toronto, who asked me which name I preferred, tested "Jimmy" to get a reaction. Once again, I said if she felt comfortable with that, then by all means, she should call me that. She continues to call me Jimmy, and from her it seems right.

Alluding to my role aboard ship as a dance host, John and Karen, from Oklahoma, call me "Bo jangles." I have no problem with that and always give them a little dance pose to acknowledge it. Another time they gave me a nickname based on something they saw on the dance floor. "Zipper Hands" was the one they came up with when they observed a lady I was dancing with pop a zipper on the back of her dress. I never got the impression they were offering either of these in a demeaning fashion; quite the contrary, I took it as a special acknowledgement.

After hearing a reading in memoir writing class about my start in the dance host business, a couple learned that on my first cruising assignment the older, more experienced hosts called me "Rookie." Now each time I see passengers Liz and Peter, one or both of them will smile and say, "Hi, Rookie." I hope they continue to do that since it provides a special connection to them I would otherwise not have had. A lady I have danced with on cruise ships many times got to calling me "Jimbo." She continues to use that nickname every time we meet. Dick, from Las Vegas, has addressed me that way for years when we meet aboard ships.

One name I have been called bewildered me. The name came from Consuelo, who lived near Mexico City. She and her friend Magdalena were always at our nightly dance sets. I would sit with them once in a while during the band's breaks. Both had great command of the English language, though they spoke to each other in Spanish. As I escorted Consuelo from the floor after a dance, she whispered, "Thank you, Santiago." When the two of them continued to address me that way, I decided I better research that a little. I discovered that the literal translation into English from Spanish was "Saint James."

One cruise line I sail with utilizes Filipinos for their wait staff, particularly in the informal eating venues. As I came through the buffet line one morning one of them, Alberto, said, "Good morning, Tiger," an obvious reference to Tiger Woods. To this day every time I see him he hits me with the "Tiger" moniker. I always try to reply with something I have heard recently about his favorite golfer.

Ross, another of these hard-working wait staff, has dubbed me "James Bond," which he annunciates in a deep, sinister voice accompanied by a broad grin. Again, that is who I am to him, though he clearly knows my name from my badge. Others of this group I know less well call me "Mr. Wood" or "Mr. James."

I began wondering about the significance, if any, of being known by multiple names. Maybe through ego or just because I am who I am, I really enjoy the variety of names I pick up from all these folks, no matter their station in life. I believe I have made some special connection with all of them in some small way. I know they have with me.

Does it really matter what form of my given name, or special nickname people call me by if it conveys a special feeling or connection between us that only we share? As a young boy, "Little Shaver," "Woodhead," and "Splinters" followed me for some time. My teenage friends called me "Woody," and I never misunderstood the implications when my mother said, "James Edmond" or my father simply called me "Wood." So call me what you choose. I'll answer.

HUSBANDS

Occasionally two or more married women will come on a cruise without their husbands. They then become unescorted ladies from our point of view, and it's their decision whether they'd like to dine or dance with us. The only rub comes when a married couple is aboard, and they have different interests. An example would be when a gentleman takes golf lessons while his wife plays bridge. In this case, a lady might wander into the dance venue while her husband is off doing something else. Seeing her alone would signal to us that she might like to dance, and a host will surely ask her. But as you can imagine, this can get tricky. Here are two situations I encountered that I wish hadn't happened.

Husband #1

An Alaskan cruise found us four dance hosts very busy. On the second evening, a group of five women came into the lounge and occupied a table near the dance floor, ordered beverages, and began to chat. I recognized one of the ladies as a travel agent I had met when she boarded with her group. When the music began, two of my fellow hosts asked two of the ladies to dance, and they graciously accepted. I was right behind them. Knowing that the travel agent would defer if I asked her, I asked the remaining lady. She accepted, and we took to the floor. About halfway through the dance, I sensed some movement near where my partner had been sitting. I adjusted my dancing so I could peek in that direction. What I saw sent chills up my spine. There stood a gentleman glaring at the dance floor, particularly at me. His hands were on his hips, and I instantly realized I was dancing with his wife. The dance ended, and I escorted her directly to him. Before he could say a word, I told him what a delightful dancer his wife was and thanked him for the privilege of dancing with her. But my attempt at disarming him was fruitless. He began to curse at me in a loud voice. Who did I think I was dancing with his wife? And on and on. With that, he took her arm and they "exited stage left." At break time, I sought out the travel agent and asked her why she hadn't warned me off or why the lady hadn't just declined my invitation. She laughed and said, "Judy has been trying to get her husband's attention for a while, and I think she finally found a way to do it."

Husband #2

Sometimes there will be dancing in the ship's theater before a show. We dance hosts station ourselves in the showroom for a dance set before the show. It was in such a situation that I asked a lady sitting alone to dance. She accepted, and we climbed the three steps to the stage that doubled as a dance floor. We had a fine dance, but as the music ended I saw a gentleman in the typical annoyed pose—hands on hips, tapping his toe—standing at the bottom of the steps. I sensed that he had been drinking, so I elected to say nothing. He proceeded to ream me out right there in the show room in front of a hundred people. "Where did I get off asking his wife to dance!" he shouted. It turns out he had sent her to save seats while he stopped in the casino. The audience could easily have taken his side, and I could really have been in hot water, though I had done nothing wrong. He continued to rant as he followed me up the aisle and I feebly tried to extricate myself from this embarrassing situation. Thankfully, he and his wife finally got to their seats. The next morning as I was walking to breakfast, I spied the same gentleman coming toward me. I had the option of turning into a cross passage but chose not to do that. If there was going to be another confrontation, this was as good a place to have it as any. As I was about to pass him, he stopped and said, "Jim, I was really out of line last night. I didn't understand that you were just doing your job of seeing that no unescorted lady was ignored." Of course, now there was no one there to hear his "heartfelt apology." I thanked him and quickly went on my way. By noontime, the situation was common gossip around the ship, and my friends were letting me know, good-naturedly, that I was in deep trouble. Taking the initiative, I sought out the cruise director and explained the whole deal. "Don't worry about it," he said with a grin. "If that's the worst thing that happens to you on this cruise, you will be indeed lucky. "It took the pressure off of me for a little while since I'm the one in hot water most of the time," he said.

GUIDE ON

Another of the rewarding duties performed by dance hosts is to act as tour escorts when the ships are in port. It gives us a chance to see the highlights of the city, while acting as a liaison between ship management and the local guide. It also gives us a chance to interact with passengers we might not otherwise get to know. I have worked with tour guides from around the world, and they are, for the most part, very articulate and informative. A few stand out in my mind for presenting some interesting behaviors that are too good to pass up:

The stunning young lady in Estonia was an out-of-work ballet dancer, and her passion for her art had to take back seat to her family's needs. At tour's end we did a little dance together in the parking lot. The hug she gave me as I left was my reward.

The male schoolteacher in South Korea was a proud and proper gentleman dressed in 1950s style. He greeted me by asking how big a tip he could expect from the passengers. He got very little.

The slightly overweight lady lawyer in St. Petersburg, Russia, gleefully admitted she did not pay any taxes on her income.

The bright and articulate young man in Zanzibar asked if I would be his sponsor so he could come to the United States. I politely declined. His disappointment was unmistakable as he shuffled off with head hung and sagged shoulders. .

The substitute school bus driver in Alaska had a husband who was a fisherman, and on strike. Dressed in denim and boots, she fit my image of what kind of people are attracted to our northern most state.

The young lady in Manaus, Brazil, asked me in a most flirtatious way, at the end of our tour, if I was free later on that evening. I didn't find out what she had in mind.

The super guide, Maurice, in Bali, hadn't worked for three months because the cruise ships quit stopping there due to terrorism within the country. I made sure all the guests on the tour knew about that.

A gentleman in Christchurch, New Zealand, had the tour bus he was driving stop at his house so he could bring his wife aboard and introduce her to us. Charming lady.

The guide at the Elephant Park in Phuket, Thailand, persuaded me to lie face down on the ground so an elephant could place one of his feet on my back. I have a picture of that.

One particular memorable experience was with a young male tour guide in Punta Arenas, Costa Rica. As a group, this country has the best tour guides and, as a result, it is one of my favorite countries. I have visited this fascinating country about six times. Peter was about twenty-five years of age and had elected the travel industry as his major field of study of study. He had graduated, served his apprenticeship, and was now a full-fledged tour guide, who spoke excellent English. The tour was an all-day affair from the port in Punta Arenas to San Jose and back. The trip to San Jose took about one and a half hours, so Peter began relating the history of his country and answering the many questions from the thirty passengers. Often he would interrupt to point out some interesting thing along the roadside. He was very knowledgeable and thorough. The only problem was one of my countrymen who was sitting on an aisle seat near the front of the bus was a constant detractor of Peter's efforts. Peter would say something like, "Costa Rica has the highest literacy rate among the Central American countries." Detractor would add, "Not as good as the US." Peter would explain that Costa Rica has no standing army. Detractor would murmur, "Probably couldn't shoot a gun anyway." This continued for some time, and although Peter couldn't help but hear these asides, he remained professional. At a rest stop, I sought Peter out and told him I understood his problem, and he assured me I didn't have to worry since he was used to that behavior. I told him I would intercede if he wanted me to. He smiled, thanked me, and said, "Not necessary."

The day went on, and Detractor lightened up a little until we were heading back to the ship. Peter was answering questions, and someone asked about coffee picking. Peter explained that it's mostly picked by Nicaraguans who are in the country legally on green cards. Detractor couldn't pass this one up and loudly wondered if the Costa Rican people were too lazy to pick the coffee themselves. Peter looked directly at him and, with no apparent animosity, said he was sure the people in California weren't lazy just because they brought in Mexicans to pick their tomatoes, or the people in the state of Washington weren't lazy just because they brought in Mexicans to pick their apples. He finished by asking the group, "Are all the workers from Mexico legally in the United States, with green cards?" A resounding "No!" erupted, and Detractor thankfully fell silent for the rest of the trip.

Ooops!

Many cruise lines conduct a meeting for entertainment department personnel early in a cruise so they can pass on new policies, the results of the last cruise, and to introduce key support staff. Normally the cruise director or his assistant conducts these meetings. Those in attendance include the production cast members, the band, and entertainment department staff members. Also invited to attend are entertainers who are aboard for a relatively short period of time. Members of the clergy, the golf pro, the instructional dance team, destination lecturers, and of course the dance hosts, fall into this category. These meetings are very informative because they give everyone a sense of the expectations of the cruise director in order to have a successful cruise.

On one occasion in 2006, on a twelve-day cruise to the Mexican Riviera, I noticed a difference in the cruise director's demeanor. He was usually really upbeat and positive. He began by telling us that the last cruise had been a near disaster. He went on to say the guests were overly demanding in general and specifically very critical of the entertainment provided. He told us the ratings were much lower than they should have been, and we could verify that by looking at them along with the written comments he'd received. From his comments and the tone of his voice, it was obvious that he expected things to get much better on this cruise.

He was just getting warmed up for what I believed to be an in-depth enumeration of his concerns when a little elderly lady sitting at the end of the third row stood up. The cruise director scanned over to her and was rewarded with this priceless comment. "Isn't this where the lecture on the Incan culture is being held?" The red-faced cruise director recovered and told her the assistant cruise director would be happy to escort her to that lecture venue. As she departed, dead silence fell upon the audience until one brave soul began to clap. We all joined in, and the cruise director quickly brightened and sheepishly said, "I guess we can't go anywhere but up from here," and dismissed the group.

The ratings for this cruise were not only better than the last cruise but were almost as high as I have ever seen in all my years of cruising.

COCOA

cruise ship's dance band varies in size depending on the needs of the ship and the need for music. Sometimes its members are drawn from the larger show band. On one particular cruise, on a smaller ship, another host and I were called upon to not only dance but also run bingo, man the spotlights for the shows, and conduct dance classes. That was fine with us and certainly no surprise to me. This upscale ship had a small lounge with cozy banquettes and a generous bar. It was equipped with a small dance floor, and three members of the show band were doing double duty playing for the nightly dancing. After every forty-five-minute set, they would exit to an anteroom to relax.

One savvy woman passenger, Tillie, only danced a few times each evening and liked to sit with one or both of us hosts and chat when we weren't dancing. She was from Canada and wore the most beautiful ensembles I'd ever seen. Without fail, each time the band would take a break she would say, "The boys are going to get some cocoa." I guessed this was her code word for their beverage of choice.

The band would always manage their last break so the last dance set of the evening would be about thirty minutes long. Almost every night the only lady left to dance with was Tillie. That's when she would look around the room and exclaim, "There doesn't appear to be any more ladies, and I'm finished dancing for the evening." That was okay with George and me. Even if there was no one to dance with, we still would be there until the official closing time. But the band didn't have to continue to play if no one was there to dance. One of them would inevitably poke his nose into the lounge to see who was left. If the only lady remaining was Tillie, he would give a little shrug and go back to his buddies and their "cocoa." One more peek into the lounge and a knowing glance and nod from Tillie told him they were dismissed for the evening. No secret as to who was running the late night music and dancing program on this ship.

A Sunday Stroll

One Sunday morning I was escorting a land tour in St. Petersburg, Russia. The group viewed the city sights by bus as our guide pointed out all the usual landmarks. The Peter and Paul Fortress, Hermitage Museum, and The Church of Our Savior were just a few of places she praised. It was time for a stop at the cruiser Aurora on the bank of the Neva River. The Aurora is famous for firing her guns to signal the start of the 1917 Russian Revolution. Led by our guide, my group boarded the cruiser, and I stationed myself ashore near the gangway. I had been on this tour several times before.

As I sipped a cup of coffee, I looked up to see two dazzling, beautiful Russian women walking leisurely nearby. I guessed them to be in their early thirties—tall, willowy, and dressed in the finest modern chic clothing. Their high heels were at least three inches, and their skirts were cut slightly above the knee revealing great-looking stems. They smiled at me as they hesitated very close by. My "good morning" rewarded me with smiles that could have melted butter. One of them responded with "Good morning" in very credible English. I asked if they were on their way to church, and they laughed heartily. That is when I realized these "ladies" were working the day shift. They quoted me the price du jour. I declined their kind invitation explaining that I was working this morning, just as they were. These two roses then sauntered slowly off with a wave over their head. I could not help but wish them success.

As my group disembarked the Aurora, one gentleman said to me, "Too bad you had to stand guard for us; you really missed a unique opportunity." If he only knew.

DREAM TEAM

Once in a great while, the hosts on a cruise really connect, and the result is amazing. This has happened to me a few times over the years but never so vividly as on a maiden cruise of a luxury liner in July 2003. Richard, Ed, Bob, and I—all seasoned hosts (code word for "older") were asked to be on this cruise from Dover, England, to New York, and on to Los Angeles. Between the four of us, we had about forty years of hosting experience, and we were all at the top of our game. We hit the floor dancing on the first evening, and a large group of ladies was waiting. We had sailed with several of them before, and that made for easy introductions and getting into the swing of things. We really pulled out all the stops, and we danced a little after the scheduled quitting time for the band. They were into it, also.

After dancing I can never just turn off the switch, so I suggested the four of us stop by one of the bars on that first evening. It was jammed with guests and staff. We found an out-of- the-way table and ordered drinks. We began to talk about all different things and found ourselves chuckling, even heartily laughing, as we shared our experiences.

The next evening after the dancing, we did the same thing and again for the next several nights. It was good to be among friends who all had the goal of making sure the passengers had a great time and who got along with each other so well. In the midst of our joking and laughing one evening, the cruise director came up to our corner table. Before we could even say hello, he said, "You guys have got to knock it off. You're having more fun than the guests." With that, he waved a waiter over and bought us a round of drinks. He departed saying that whatever we were doing to keep doing it. We had no trouble following that advice for the rest of the cruise, and everyone—the ladies, the band, and the cruise director—were happy. We hosts were the happiest of all, with or without the after-hours libations.

HELPFUL, I HOPE

In my experience as a host, I have found that most times things are really black and white. But not so with Roger from San Francisco, who was one of my tablemates on a fourteen-day cruise out of Sydney, Australia, in January 2004. He was an enigma wrapped in a riddle inside a puzzle. I pride myself on being able to read people fairly quickly and accurately. That trait comes in very handy as I perform my host duties and has kept me from sticking my foot in my mouth a few times. Roger was a handsome gentleman, who dressed impeccably and sported a smile most of the time. In conversations, he was articulate and well informed on current events. His questions to me and our fellow tablemates were polite and showed a genuine interest as he soaked in the many details of our backgrounds, homes, families, and experiences. But when we asked him anything personal, he quickly changed the subject, artfully asking a question of the questioner.

Four single ladies were at our table, and it was obvious they were very interested to know more about this elusive tablemate. On several occasions, one or the other would ask me about Roger, and I had to confess I was as clueless as they were. Cindy from Portland, Oregon, told me she checked the guest book and found out that Roger was from San Francisco. But he had already told us that.

About four days into the cruise, I ran into Roger at lunch, and he asked me to join him. As we chatted, I sensed he had something on his mind. I took the initiative and offered that he and I were lucky guys to have four ladies at our table. He agreed but added that he had a small problem that maybe I could help him with. He told me that he had a great interest in a different lady he had met who was seated near us at dinner. He sensed she was likewise inclined, but he was unsure how to proceed. He admitted that he was not sharing too much about himself for fear it would further pique the interest of the ladies at our table. Well, he had that right, I thought.

I suggested he make a reservation at one of the specialty restaurants and invite this special lady. If she accepted, he would be off to a flying start at getting to know her. If he did not show up at our table, I would tell the ladies he was dining with an old friend who he hadn't seen for some time. He thanked me and, as I guessed, he was absent from the table that very evening and several others thereafter. The ladies readily accepted my explanation for Roger's absence. Being astute, they concentrated their attention someone some other eligible gentlemen. Each year, I receive a Christmas card from Roger (and his new wife), and I still smile when I think of our little secret.

CABIN SHARING

As part of our dance host contract, we acknowledge that we may have to share a cabin with another host when necessary. Though the cabins tend to be rather small for two persons, this is not normally a problem. I have shared with some hosts whose behaviors in that regard were, shall we say, interesting.

In April 1996, I was booked on two ten-day cruises in and out of San Francisco to the Mexican Riviera. When I arrived at my cabin I found George, my fellow host, rearranging the furniture to maximize the distance between the twin beds. Maybe he thought I was gay. He did this by putting both the twelve-inch bedside tables between the beds. This required moving one of the beds (mine) twelve inches closer to the closet with sliding doors that we were sharing. George always seemed to secure his clothes from the closet at the least convenient time for me. Being a newer kid on the host block, I tolerated this for one of the two cruises but finally suggested that the least George could do was trade beds for the next cruise. He reluctantly agreed, and on the second morning when I returned to the cabin the room arrangement was back to what it was originally. I never said a word about it, and neither did he.

I pegged cabin mate Calvin as a self-serving type when I first met him. It did not take him long to prove me right. As part of our deal with the cruise line, we get free laundry service if we choose, or can use the washers and dryers that are strategically located throughout the ship. Calvin elected to wash some of his clothes in the bathroom basin. He then attached his washed socks, underwear, sports shirts, and handkerchiefs to a line he strung around our cabin. A laundry line stretched from our common mirror, to a wall picture, across the drapery rod, and ended on a nail that Calvin had anchored on the wall molding at ceiling level. The colored plastic clothespins he used to hang his clothes were a nice touch. Thankfully, he had only placed the line with clothing across his two-thirds of the space. As I pondered how to approach Calvin, the problem solved itself. Apparently, our cabin stewardess reported the condition to her supervisor, who in turn alerted the cruise director. Calvin was ordered to remove the wash line and utilize the proper facilities. I believe he thought I had complained and since I was about to, I never bothered to tell him I had not.

John, from California, was a really great-looking guy with a nice tan who just oozed sex appeal. When we first met, he made no bones about his proclivity for extracurricular activities with any willing lady on the cruise. Since we were cabin mates I sensed, correctly, that he was forewarning me of the possibility of a successful campaign on his part that would affect our living arrangements. It was 2003, and I had been a host for nearly fifteen years, so I was not a naïve rookie. We hosts know that paying extra attention to ladies is verboten, but John seemed not to care. Of course being a willing accomplice to his actions could cause me problems as well. So when he approached me about five days into a fourteen-day cruise from Barcelona to Rome with the request that I absent myself from the cabin for a couple of hours that night after our dancing, I said, "No way." He gave me the old, "Come on, friend, don't ruin my fun routine," but I didn't waver. He told me he would inform the cruise director he needed his own cabin because I was gay. Needless to say, this really pissed me off. I told him that would be a huge mistake for I, in turn, would give my side of the story to the cruise director, including the name of the lady I was sure he had selected, and also e-mail our agent explaining his modus operandi. I suggested that if he was bound and determined to go through with his liaison, he should go to the lady's cabin. To this day I don't know how or if he solved his dilemma, but I didn't hear any more about me vacating our shared accommodations.

BACKLEAD

Often the ladies we dance with are used to dancing with their husbands. Since the typical husband is not an accomplished dancer, their wives get in the habit of leading. This makes it easy for the husband since he is pushed and pulled from one part of the floor to another without having to know much more than a few basic steps. His biggest challenge is to find reasons *not* to dance. Thus it becomes an interesting challenge when we hosts dance with these ladies. (Dare I call them "leading ladies?"?) They have trouble following our lead and become tentative, stiff, and sometimes defensive. It is our job to try to make them feel at ease and provide an enjoyable experience.

Jolene, a divorcee from Tulsa, was one of these ladies. Immediately upon beginning our first dance, she announced that she was used to leading. I told her I noticed that. I said that she really wasn't leading, but back leading, and tried to explain the difference. "If you really want to lead, then you need me to take the lady's position and you the gentleman's," I pointed out. "I know I can follow you, so give it your best shot," I said. We positioned ourselves, and I told her to start. The look on her face told me that starting with her left foot forward, as the leader does, was confusing her. We chuckled, and I took over as the leader for the rest of the dance. Afterward, I told her if she would follow me by mid cruise, she would enjoy it. Over the next several days we did just that, and she did wonderful. She also allowed my fellow dance hosts to lead. She and I laughed about how she had wasted so many years not having fun dancing with her husband. She confided in me that they had taken lessons but since she was taking the back lead role, her husband wasn't able to learn his role correctly. As I had promised, by mid cruise she was indeed having fun and dancing quite well. At cruise end she thanked me and wondered if when she got back home and went to her singles' dances whether she would be able to resist her back lead technique. Lead on no more, Jolene!

WE TOOK TOOK A TUK TUK

The port was Cochin, India, and it was a day off for us hosts. Though what we do is mostly fun, a little time away from the guests, the ship, and our daily routine is always appreciated. Bob and I didn't have to be back aboard until late afternoon, so we decided to go on an adventure. We left the ship around 10:00 a.m. knowing we had lots of time to explore this city of six million in southwest India. On advice of the onboard concierge, we decided that a "tuk tuk" would be an appropriate form of transportation. A tuk tuk is a three-wheeled enclosed vehicle that uncomfortably holds a driver and two back-seat passengers. The concierge gave us the names of two hotel restaurants where we could have a great lunch. We went through the required immigration procedure for disembarking and had our boarding passes reviewed and stamped by Indian authorities at the gangway. Then we had our ship ID scanned, we walked down the ramp, and showed our India documents again to officials. Since the Mumbai terrorist attack on November 26, 2008, sometimes referred to as 26/11, security has toughened. Finally we walked about two hundred feet and found the lineup of taxis and tuk tuks. I negotiated a round-trip fee, payable upon return for a tuk tuk to take us to one of the fine hotels suggested. We planned to do a little shopping and have lunch. We didn't realize it at the time, but it was Sunday, and the shops were closed. So our driver set off to the Anchor House Hotel. Our tuk tuk driver, Sargent, was a master of dodging and weaving as we sped off at high speed. Traffic converged on us from all angles. Taxis, cars, trucks, buses, bicycles, and people seemed to come out of nowhere. Somehow Sargent negotiated this chaos using a blaring horn that blended in all the others. Sargent was married to a fine woman named Jasmine, he said. They had two grown daughters. One was a civil engineer and the other a computer programmer. I engaged Sargent in conversation most of the way, asking him questions about a variety of things. I did this for two reasons: to get a sense of his English, and to establish a comfort level with his city and its points of interest. He gave a running narration as we putted past the famous Chinese fishing nets, the naval base, and the girls' academy.

Finally, we arrived at the hotel where Brian, the manager, and Archana, the hostess greeted us. Archana was the most beautiful Indian girl I had ever seen. Fashionably dressed in an ornate long dress, tastefully applied makeup, and long graceful manicured fingernails, her beauty was breathtaking. Her flashing smile and quiet charm would disarm the most sullied of people. She and Brian were the official welcoming committee. After a tour of this small hotel and its facilities, Brian escorted us to a second-floor table overlooking the harbor. Bob and I ordered an appetizer and cold Kingfisher beers as we relaxed and took in the sights and sounds. The overhead fans bathed us in a cool breeze that sheltered us from the otherwise hot and humid climate. The tasty starters of fried cheese bits and chicken were followed by an order of grilled shrimp for me and a local fish dish for Bob. We talked with a delightful couple from Wales at the next table, Ian and Julia, who were on a one hundred eight-day world cruise aboard a ship moored adjacent to ours. They were delightful, and we exchanged cruising experiences for nearly an hour.

Time passed quickly, and soon it was time to return to our home away from home. Before we left we had our pictures taken with Brian and Archana using my camera. I promised to e-mail copies to them, which I did at my first opportunity. Back aboard our tuk tuk, Sargent negotiated city traffic and returned us safely to the ship. I paid him the agreed-upon fare, and we left him with a smile and a wave. Total time away from the ship was six hours. Total cost for appetizers, lunch, beverages, tips, and a thrill ride worthy of Epcot was twenty-four dollars each. We were able to relax for a while, and we had great food to eat. We interacted with folks we wouldn't ordinarily meet. That's what I liked about a day with my friend Bob in India.

SIGNAL SYSTEM

The dance bands on the cruise lines I have sailed with are truly unique. Whether a trio, sextet, or something else, they do a fine job. It is not easy to play song after song, night after night, cruise after cruise, while staying fresh and maintaining an upbeat attitude. The dance bands I'm familiar with are on contracts of six months or so, and that means the members are away from home and family for that period. Though I'm normally with them for three or four cruises, I always appreciate the efforts of the guys whose music makes us look good. I make it a point to introduce myself to them early on and spend at least a few minutes with them nightly. I never fail to thank them at the end of each evening's dance. I have sailed with bands whose members are Polish, English, and American, but the ones I like best and get to know well are the Filipinos. In our little chats, they never fail to ask if there is any special music I would like them to play. It is more than just politeness on their part, for they know some dance hosts can be critical, so they are really interested in our opinion. I always assure them that they are playing fine. I tell them, from time to time, I would like to dance a certain dance with a lady, not because she has asked but because I happen to know she likes it.

I have devised a little hand signaling system that I can use discreetly to let the band know I'd like them to play a certain type of song. A time-out sign, or T, signals I want them to play a tango. A "C" is for cha-cha; three fingers pointing up is a waltz; three fingers pointing down is a mambo; and a swaying of my head from side-to- side indicates a swing. I don't use these signals often, maybe twice in an evening. I will quickly flash one of my signs before the bandleader has decided exactly what song they will play next. This gives them a chance to make the change if they see me. If not, no big deal. But when it works it's a blast, and the smiles from the band members about our little secret shows they appreciate this little diversion. If I don't give them a signal for a few evenings, they wonder what's wrong.

Over the years I have seen some of these same bands, at least their leader, on subsequent cruises. On the first night, a band member who I have sailed with before never fails to flash me one of the dance signs as I approach him. We laugh, and I know I am off to another good start with this band. I don't let them down, for I'll make sure to give them a sign early on that first night.

Dos Señoras

T hough I've met hundreds of people as a dance host for the cruise lines, there are several who have really touched me, even though they have not made spectacular impacts on the human condition. Neither have they had some overpowering physical magnetism. Rather they just strike some chord within me, and I can't or won't let them go. So it was with two ladies from Tampico, Mexico.

Mari was short, dark-haired, plain-faced, and matronly in appearance. What set her apart from the masses were her dark, nearly black eyes that missed nothing. A look from her would penetrate your very being in one moment and exude the kindness of a saint in the next. She had been a widow for forty-six years when I met her on a cruise from Mumbai, India, to Dover, England. Mari's traveling friend was Magdalena, who was tall, fashion conscious, with carefully styled hair, and had the demeanor of a patient grandmother. She had been separated from her husband some twenty-three years earlier. Her strong Catholic upbringing prevented the final severing of their long-dead relationship, she told me. She talked about her grandchildren, and they obviously were a big part of her life.

I met them early in the cruise and danced with them every evening. They would arrive at the dance venue, sit at a table by themselves, and sip tequila. They never refused a dance, no matter what the song. Though they were not very good dancers, they smiled and chatted with us hosts as we danced. I learned that they did not lack a sense of humor as they laughed at their dancing faults. Among the last to leave every night, they seemed to be having a great time.

Later in the cruise I was seated at their dining table, and I learned much more about them. They were cousins and had grown up together. Also, they shared a very strong religious conviction and attended Mass every morning. Their children, grandchildren, and relatives had anointed both of them as the matriarchs of their families. After all, they told me, that is the role you are cast into when you are older and have no husband in "their Mexico." That being the case, they had no social life aside from their families. Dinner or a movie with a gentleman would be unthinkable, they said. They did, however, take two or three getaways together during the year. No wonder they enjoyed this very safe, though temporary, encounter with us dance hosts. Magdalena confided in me that it was nice to have a man around. She said Mari agreed, but would never say it.

Each day brought me new respect and a genuine special feeling for these ladies. They began to call me "Santiago" instead of James, which had been their regular greeting. The way they spoke, it was more like I would expect them to address a true friend, and I believe that is what I became. They even offered to treat me to a tequila shooter! Of course, I accepted.

COURTEOUS CURTSEY?

Sometimes what you see is not what you get. In March 2012, I was a dance host on a ship sailing for fifty-seven days up the Pacific Rim, then the Aleutian Islands, and down the West Coast of the United States, ending in Los Angeles. These were three separate cruises, which were part of a five-segment world cruise on a very upscale cruise line. We eight hosts were kept very busy, and thing were going smoothly. The ladies we were dancing with were happy, and the dance team we reported to was happy, as was the cruise director. Since we were in this part of the world, we had a great number of Asian ladies who wished to dance. Many of them were Japanese, and although there was a little language barrier we all made things work, and it appeared all was going well.

One Japanese lady, Yuko, was a pint-sized bundle of energy that greeted us at the first dance set nightly at 5:15 p.m. and left us at the end of the dancing at 12:30 a.m. Though just a fair dancer, she certainly made up for her lack of dancing skills with her glorious smile and the curtsey she performed at the end of each and every dance. Things went well until midway into our last cruise segment. It was early evening, and for the first time, Yuko was not there when the band started to play. The one other lady present requested that she have her pictures taken on deck with us hosts. We obliged and were gone from the dance area for perhaps two or three minutes. We reentered the dance floor only to see Yuko taking off from the area. Little did we suspect she was reporting our absence to the front desk, who in turn reported that fact to the dance team. Within minutes Yuko returned and began to berate us, in fairly good English, for not being available to dance when she arrived. She wouldn't accept any explanation, and she even took off on the other lady for taking us away from our dancing duties.

We three hosts tried to explain the situation to her as best we could, but she just wasn't having it. I knew that we would hear about this sooner or later, and I was right. The very next day, the dance team we reported to advised us of the complaint. We explained what had transpired and were assured that it was okay, but to be careful of this lady.

I must admit that our enthusiasm for dancing with Yuko waned somewhat after that, although we made sure she was not slighted when it was her turn. We still got the smile and the curtsey after each dance, but it certainly didn't mean the same to me as it once had. As a postscript to this, we learned that Yuko actually counted the number of dances that were played one night and the number that she was invited to dance. Her count was fifty-two total dances one evening, and she danced thirty of them, courtesy of the hosts.

I Miss You Already

In February 1997, I was sailing from Sydney, Australia, to Hong Kong. I was one of six hosts, and we had a pretty full ship with plenty of ladies to dance and socialize with. Among the unescorted lady passengers was a group from the Columbus, Ohio area. Through the stops at Melbourne, Adelaide, and Fremantle, we got to know them pretty well. It soon became apparent that I was more interested in one of these super ladies than the others. Her name was Pat. This was not only a new feeling for me but one we hosts must guard against since it is our duty to treat each lady equally.

I now faced the dilemma of doing my job while also allowing the lady in question to know I had more than a passing interest in her. Without making a big deal about it, I explained to Pat the role of a dance host. Since this was her first cruise, she thanked me for the information. We were able to spend some time together with another host and three other ladies, so I did get to know her a little better. Of course, I got to dance with her, and that kindled my interest as well. On a few land tours I escorted, I noticed that Pat and her friend Nancy would try to get aboard the bus I was on. I even got some pictures of them. I still was feeling a little guilty even though I was convinced I was officially not paying more attention to her than the other ladies. By the time we got to Hong Kong, we were more than casual friends, and we had exchanged names, addresses, and phone numbers. Another host and I escorted Pat and Nancy on a walking tour of Hong Kong, including Mt. Victoria. It was there, out of the sight of other ships' guests, that we were able to sit down over lunch and a glass of wine and really get to talk to each other. I found myself feeling very much alive and comfortable with this recently widowed lady.

The next day was disembarkation in Hong Kong, and as usual, I positioned myself near the gangway to wish the passengers well as they left the ship. As the Columbus ladies left, I wished them all well. When it came Pat's turn to leave, I gave her a little hug and said, "I miss you already."

I, too, was leaving the ship that day and flying home. I had a layover of several hours in San Francisco, and while there I called Pat and caught her just as she was walking into her home. Right then and there, we set up a time for me to visit, and within ten days I was able to give her my undivided attention.

It has now been over fourteen years since we met, and Pat and I are still going strong. By mutual agreement, we have no marriage plans, but we visit each other on a regular basis and travel together to many wonderful places on vacations. Pat recently retired from the business her late husband had founded and doesn't need or want me around full-time. That's okay because my feelings for her don't require being together 24/7.

Unknown Gift

As a dance host, I have opportunities to tap into the vast travel experiences of others. As I listen to them tell of the places they've been and where they intend to go, my mind whirls. Since I have made it my life's goal in my golden years to travel as far and wide as possible, this kind of input is invaluable. I can't get enough of it. People who have not traveled much tend to glaze over when those who have talk about the places they have visited and the sights they've seen. In fact, I make it a point not to go into too much detail at home when friends ask where I've been "now." Their use of that word sends the message to me. They're interested, but only politely. On the other hand, people who have traveled listen attentively, as I do, when their fellow globetrotters relate their experiences.

From Gerry and Dawne, on a cruise across the Atlantic, I learned of an upscale restaurant in Cape Town, South Africa. I went to that restaurant and was treated to the most delicious meal of Portobello mushrooms stuffed with crabmeat and a main course of springbok, a deer-like native animal. They also recommended a Pinotage red wine, which was excellent. That wine now is a standard in my home. I have since returned there, with Pat.

While sunning on an upper deck on a cruise, I overheard people talking about a riverboat cruise on the Danube River. I engaged them in a conversation about their tour, and they gladly supplied the details of their trip. They also recommended a travel company that offered attractive packages for this adventure. Based on what I heard and their enthusiasm, my friend Pat and I booked one from Bucharest to Amsterdam and both agreed it was a highlight of our travels.

Dolores, a delightful dancer and world traveler, told me of her wonderful experience on an extended land trip in New Zealand. Her descriptions of the two islands were intriguing. She extolled the friendliness of the people and their laid-back approach to life. Intrigued with that combination, Pat and I endured the seventeen-hour flight to investigate. Dolores was right; we found a two-week itinerary there based mostly on her say so. From whomever they are to wherever they've been, these folks, and many more I've had the pleasure of meeting, have bestowed upon me a gift unknown to them, and I'll be ever thankful.

CHANGE WATER INTO WINE

After years of cruising as a host, I rarely get rattled or fall victim to my own errant behavior, but it happened big time in the fall of 2005 when Pat and I took a river cruise from Bucharest to Amsterdam. This twenty-eight-day excursion was most delightful. The riverboat carried one hundred twenty guests, and meals were open seating. This gave everyone a chance to dine with different people if they wanted to. Pat and I have always enjoyed doing this, and during the first several days we got to know many different people.

One particular evening, we entered the dining room, and two couples asked us to join them. Before long we were chatting and having a wonderful time. Pat and I enjoy wine with dinner, and on this cruise each dinner was to include two glasses of wine "of your choice." All tables were set with standard water glasses, a pitcher of ice water, and smaller wine glasses. Early in the cruise, Pat and I thought it would be cute to fill our wine glass with water, leaving the larger water glass free to be filled with wine by our waiter. We did this only when we dined alone, but unbeknownst to us it had not gone unnoticed. Of course, since we were guests at the table this evening, we were not about to do our wine routine.

One of the gentlemen, Craig, asked us if we wanted water, and we said yes. I handed him my water glass and he said, "No, give me the other glass." Without hesitation, I handed him Pat's water glass. He smiled and said, "No, the wine glasses, please." Again, without batting an eye, I passed the two wine glasses to him, which he dutifully filled with water and passed back to us. He did the same with the other couples' wine glasses, his wife's, and his own. Of course, when the server poured the wine we all got it in our water glasses. No words were spoken, and the dinner progressed nicely. At its end, we all bid each other a good evening and departed.

The next evening when we arrived for dinner, our new friends had saved a spot for us and asked us once again to join them. Before we could scoot our chairs to the table, they related this story to us. Apparently our glass-switch maneuver had been observed by these four for some time. They all agreed they had to meet these mischievous people who were getting more wine than they without breaking the rules. They had decided to invite us to join them and see how that worked out. We all had a good laugh, although it was somewhat of an embarrassing one for Pat and me. They asked if we would like to share their table at dinner for the rest of the trip. How could we refuse? Waiter, fill 'er up!

SMALL WORLD

Early in 2007, I was an assigned as a host on a cruise starting in Los Angeles and ending in Buenos Aires, Argentina. Shortly after embarking, I was made aware that three people from my part of the country were aboard. Anytime I'm on a ship I always check to see if any of the passengers are from Pennsylvania. I have found over the years that California is the state with the highest percentage of cruisers, at least on the ships I sail. Though I had met passengers from Pennsylvania before, it is not the norm. When I do, I make sure to look them up at the earliest possible opportunity. It makes me feel good to have a home connection, and I hope it does the same for them. A check of the passenger list turned up no names from my state. But during a meeting for the oncoming staff, a lady and gentleman approached me sporting huge smiles. It was Joe and Maria, and their home was about twenty minutes from mine. It turned out Joe was a guest lecturer, and his topic was "Memoir Writing." His wife, Maria, and daughter Claire were with him for this once-in-a-lifetime experience. They were delighted to see someone from home, and as time permitted, we got to know each other.

I decided to attend one of Joe's lectures and became fascinated with his easygoing style of assuring everyone that writing a memoir was not that difficult. Additionally, he conducted workshops where you could get personal help. I became really enthusiastic because I had often thought about doing something like Joe was talking about. Though I didn't make a commitment at the time, it kept nagging at me. I enjoyed what time I could spare with Joe and his family, and we all became good friends. We promised to get in touch when we got back home. We did, and Joe and Maria invited me to their home for dinner one summer evening. I told them of my memoir plan, and mostly because of their urging, early in 2005 I wrote a story for my twenty-year-old granddaughter covering my life from the time I could remember up to my graduation from high school. The "manuscript" grew and grew and took me until December of that year to finish. I presented it to Samantha for Christmas that year.

Joe, Maria, and I found ourselves on a cruise together again in 2008. The response to Joe and his memoir presentation had been such a huge hit with the passengers that he was invited back to teach again. This time, in addition to Maria, he had brought his son Paul. I shared with Joe that I had been writing little snippets about people, places, and behaviors since I started hosting in 1989. I said I had quite a collection and that I enjoyed reviewing them from time to time to reminisce.

In the winter of 2011, Joe and Maria were at sea again on a world cruise. This time Joe and Maria were the yoga instructors, and Joe continued with his popular memoir-writing class. He organized special sessions where stories that his students had written were presented. He asked (and I consented) to having two of my pieces read. "Ghost Host" and "Alfred the Great" were among those presented by the ship's entertainment staff. After those readings and the positive response they got from the audience, Joe told me that with all the years of cruising experience I have had, there had to be a book in there somewhere. Joe offered to put fresh eyes and ears to my efforts, which I am now eternally grateful for. I had not recognized the goldmine of experiences I had been gathering during my travels. But he did. This book is the product of my efforts with Joe's urging, helpful hints, and patience.

THE SHIP MOVES ON

S itting at home one evening in 2009, I received a phone call from a fellow host alerting me that one of our colleagues, Peter, had been stricken with a heart attack while at sea. It turned out that at the next port (Acapulco, Mexico), he was transferred to a local hospital, and the ship moved on. The next day, he died in a place far away from his home and family. I wondered if he had wished to be cared for at a hospital near his home with loved ones by his side, but of course that had not happened.

I remember hearing that another host friend, Jim, whose passion was to see every country in the world, had passed away while aboard a cruise ship seeking to fulfill that dream. He, too, had been away from home, family, and friends when he died. He was transferred to shore at the next port for his final trip home, and the ship moved on.

In both cases, these hosts had spent a great deal of their golden years doing what they loved—traveling the world. I have firsthand knowledge of their love of travel and the benefits of sampling other cultures, peoples, and landscapes. I can understand very well why these two friends continued to travel even as they got older and maybe a little less healthy. Though I'm sure everything possible was done to save Peter and Jim, they died alone in unfamiliar surroundings, and the ship moved on.

The reward of travel makes me feel happy, engaged, and worthwhile, yet it is always balanced against the risk of being alone, or even lonely, from time to time, and that is very sad. But that is okay with me since I believe we come into this world alone, and we may go out alone. I do have some fears because of my traveling lifestyle. I fear I won't take time to share my traveling experiences with my granddaughters. I fear I won't be able to tell my sons how much I love them and appreciate their attention to me in my senior years. I fear I won't adequately pass on to family members the lessons I have learned from my life experiences that they may benefit them. It's my intent that this book helps do that.

Hopefully, when my life is ended, whether at sea or at home, I'll not feel lonely because I had taken the time to share my innermost thoughts with those closest to me. I will continue to travel the world as much as I can, since that is my life's goal in my senior years. I will always keep in mind one thing: The ships always keep moving on.

16378163R00156

Made in the USA
Charleston, SC
17 December 2012